שיעורי הרב

Shiurei HaRav

A Conspectus of the Public Lectures
of Rabbi Joseph B. Soloveitchik

שיעורי הרב

Shiurei HaRav

A Conspectus of the Public Lectures
of Rabbi Joseph B. Soloveitchik

Edited by
Joseph Epstein

KTAV Publishing House, Inc.
Hoboken, NJ

Contributing editors:

Shalom Carmy
Dov Kanner
Menachem Kasdan
Ezra Labaton
Joel B. Wolowelsky

Library of Congress Cataloging -in-Publication Data

Soloveitchik, Joseph Dov.
    Shiurei HaRav = [Shi'ure ha-Rav] : a conspectus of the public lectures of
Rabbi Joseph B. Soloveitchik / edited by Joseph Epstein.
In English; some essays translated from Hebrew or Yiddish.
        p.   cm.
    ISBN 0-88125-499-1
    1. Judaism. I. Title. II. Title: Shiu'ure ha-Rav.
BM45.S67 1994
296—dc20   94-10838
                                                                CIP

Manufactured in the United States of America

KTAV Publishing House, Inc., 900 Jefferson St., Hoboken, NJ, 07030

Contents

Publisher's Foreword

The Torah world is just coming to terms with the void left by the death of Rabbi Joseph B. Soloveitchik, *zt"l*. Over the decades, the Rav—the simple title by which he was known to his students and followers—shaped Torah Judaism in the United States and around the world, combining a vast knowledge of rabbinic scholarship with a sensitivity to and understanding of Western civilization. One of the *gedolei doreinu*, the Torah giants of our generation, the Rav was rebbe to thousands of students who have carried his Torah to tens of thousands of others.

For many years, the Rav's Torah was primarily an oral one. He published little, and personal access to his thought was limited for the most part to those who attended his Talmud sh'urim at Yeshiva University, his weekly Saturday night Bible sh'urim in Boston, his annual T'shuva lectures in New York, his yearly Yahrzeit addresses, or his infrequent talks on college campuses.

Gradually, his Torah took on written form. Some of his extensive essays in Hebrew and English were published, many in *Hadarom* and *Tradition* or as separate books. Pinchas Peli published extensive summaries of many of his Yiddish T'shuva lectures in Hebrew and English versions, and, more recently, Moshe Kroner offered the aggada portions of some of his Yiddish Yahrzeit sh'urim in Hebrew. Rabbi Abraham Besdin has published an extensive collection of reconstructions in English of the Rav's public lectures. Rabbis Menachem Genack and Hershel Schachter have begun publishing short *hiddushim* of the Rav, and Rabbi Heshie Reichmann has published extensive notes of the Rav's sh'urim on Massekhtot Sukkah and Shavuot. Lawrence Kaplan provided an English translation of the Rav's classics, *Halakhic Man* and *Kol Dodi Dofek*.

But twenty years ago, all that was available to the general public were a few published pieces by the Rav and privately circulated notes of his lectures and classes. The editors of *Hamevaser*, Yeshiva University's student Torah newspaper, recognized the growing thirst for their Rebbe's Torah and published *Shiurei HaRav*. They provided the first English version of some of the Rav's published Hebrew and Yiddish essays and offered extensive epitomes of some twenty of his sheurim and lectures.

Long out of print, *Shiurei HaRav* is now being reissued by KTAV in continued recognition of the Rav's manifold contribution to the worldwide Torah community. Summaries of lectures which the Rav subsequently published in full have been eliminated, as the actual texts are now available. "Kodesh and Hol," an out-of-print essay that appeared in the 1966 issue of *Gesher*, a Torah publication of the Student Organization of Yeshiva, has been included, as has been "The Nine Aspects of the Haggada," which appeared in the Student Organization of Yeshiva Haggada. We are grateful to Yeshiva University for permission to reprint the material.

We also extend our heartfelt thanks to Mrs. Els Bendheim, who brought *Shiurei HaRav* to our attention.

Preface

Rabbi Joseph B. Soloveitchik, the man of halakha, is universally recognized as one of the major Jewish leaders and philosophers of our time. His ideas and thoughts have influenced large segments of the world Jewish community, so much so that the simple appellation "The Rav" is taken to refer to Rabbi Soloveitchik. Unfortunately, because of family tradition, the Rav has been reluctant to publish his works, and much of what he says is heard by only the limited audiences attending his public lectures and *shiurim*. His Torah is therefore a *Torah she-b'al Peh*—an oral Torah and law.

Over the past several years private notes and reconstructions of Rabbi Soloveitchik's lectures have increasingly been made available to a wider audience. HAMEVASER has consistently performed such a unique service. Most of the Rav's public lectures at Yeshiva University have been featured on our pages. The Rabbinical Council of America has recently published a series of journalistic reconstructions of the Rav's lectures under the editorship of Rabbi Abraham R. Besdin. Other successful projects have been undertaken, primarily in the Boston area, to spread the ideas and teachings of Rabbi Soloveitchik.

This present publication goes beyond all previous efforts. We have undertaken this project in the hope of introducing Rabbi Soloveitchik's thoughts and ideas to an even larger audience.

In part I we have featured a brief introduction to the Rav's weltanschauung along with a biographical sketch.

In part II we present selections of Rabbi Soloveitchik's writings and lectures which have appeared in print but have not been widely circulated. Two essays were adapted from the original Hebrew and one from the original Yiddish. The fourth lecture is reproduced from the English source with the subsequent emendations requested by the Rav.

In the Part III we present synopses (based upon students' notes) of a selection of the public lectures given by the Rav primarily during the last decade. The divisions within this part are arbitrary and were instituted for the convenience of the reader. There is certainly a great deal of overlap in the thoughts and ideas expressed in all the sections.

Rabbi Soloveitchik makes his home in Boston and commutes weekly to New York City, where he gives three advanced Talmud *shiurim* at Yeshiva University and one Talmud *shiur* for the general public at Congregation Moriah in midtown Manhattan. In Boston, the Rav lectures every *motza'ei shabbat* (Saturday night) at the Maimonides Yeshiva.

These lectures on *Ḥumash* are regularly attended by hundreds of students and laymen in the Boston area and a summary of three of these classes is reconstructed in this volume (*Aseret ha-Dibrot*). On Sunday morning in Boston, the Rav also gives another Talmud class.

Over the past decade, the Rav's annual *t'shuva d'rashot* have become an important part of the high holiday experience of many people in the New York city area. Delivered in Yiddish, the lectures are published the following year in an extensive Hebrew adaptation in the Israeli magazine *Panim El Panim.* We present here two adopted examples of these lectures.

At Yeshiva University, Rabbi Soloveitchik has for the past several years delivered an annual lecture in observance of the yahrzeits of his late wife, Mrs. Tonya Soloveitchik *z"l,* and his late brother, Dr. Samuel Soloveitchik *z"l.* Delivered in English, usually in the week preceding Purim, these lectures have usually dealt with the Purim holiday. They attract a

large crowd of students, alumni, faculty, and guests from
the entire New York metropolitan area. We have printed
several synopses of these lectures in this volume.

On a number of occasions, Rabbi Soloveitchik has addressed
students from campuses other than Yeshiva College. In 1962,
he spoke at the MIT Hillel, in 1972 at Stern College, and in
1973 at Rutgers. Similarly, the Rav addressed students of the
Yolanda Benson Honor Society of YU on the topic "The
Unique Experience of Judaism" in 1972. All these lectures
are presented in this booklet.*

The Rav maintains a close relationship with many American
Orthodox rabbis who have studied under his guidance. He
periodically addresses the Rabbinic Alumni of Yeshiva
University and the Rabbinical Council of America. Several of
these lectures are featured in this book.

Of course, the Rav's major contribution is his daily Talmud
shiur given at Yeshiva University. Because of their technical
halakhic nature, these classes are clearly beyond the scope
of this philosophical conspectus. However, we do present,
as the last article in this volume, the Rav's impromptu remarks
to his class at the *siyyum* (completion) of a chapter of
Tractate *Hullin*. It is interesting to note that when the Rav
lectures before an audience well versed in halakha, the
philosophical concepts he develops are rooted in technical
halakhic constructs, as may be seen in this article and the
t'shuva lectures.

It must be made clear the lectures reprinted in this volume
are on the whole not literal reproductions. They are primarily
reconstructions from notes or synopses of the original lectures.
Since they are in this form, all weaknesses and defects are
the fault of HAMEVASER and the individual author.

This volume should in no way be misconstrued to be the
official or authoritative representation of Rabbi Soloveitchik's
works. It in no ways claims to portray or delineate the

scope of Rabbi Soloveitchik's thoughts. Our purpose is twofold: to organize several of Rabbi Soloveitchik's essays and lectures into a single booklet so that some of his ideas will become more widely circulated, and to serve as a guide or reference book for the many people who have heard Rabbi Soloveitchik during one of the many lectures reprinted here.

Of course nothing can substitute for being at the Rav's lectures. The eloquence of expression, the art of sculpturing concrete verbal images in such precise detail that they seem a reality, the soaring poetry of a visionary, the mood--evoking magic of an extraordinary storyteller, and, finally, the ability to fashion a bond of existential fellowship among all those present--and anyone who has ever heard the Rav speak knows how well he does all of these—cannot be captured in this volume.

Because we have collected articles from diverse sources, we encountered the difficult problem of standardizing the several unique systems of transliterations in use. In all cases in the reprinted articles, we followed the prevailing system in use in that specific article.

Many people have worked very diligently and devotedly in the preparation of this special publication. Many thanks must be extended to Menachem Kasdan for freely giving of his ideas, literary talents, and time; to Joel Wolowelsky for his initial spark and continued advice and guidance in this project; to Ezra Labaton for his insights, suggestions, and time; to Dov Kanner for his extraordinary efforts and work in reviewing and proofreading this entire booklet; and to Shalom Carmy for freely giving of his erudition and for sharing with us his polyglot expertise.

Particular note must be made of the efforts of Moshe Rand in reviewing sections of this book. David Derovan's help and guidance in the various technical aspects of this book have been indispensable. The manifold efforts and the helpful suggestions of Ephraim Buchwald were greatly appreciated.

It is well apparent that the individual writers of this volume did an excellent job in their assignments. To them is due the greatest thanks and appreciation for their efforts.

Much gratitude must be expressed to the Governing Board and the special edition staff of HAMEVASER for their diligence and dedication in all the major and minor facets of this publication.

The greatest admiration and esteem must be shown to Rabbi Soloveitchik for his efforts and leadership in the Jewish community. Throughout the world, thousands of his students and admirers look to their rebbe and mentor for his inspiration and guidance. It has been our great fortune to be allowed to undertake this project. We hope we have been successful in presenting these ideas of Judaism, the spirit of the Torah, and the *Torat ha-Rav* to our readers.

Joseph Epstein
Editor-in-Chief
Iyar 5734—May 1974
Yeshiva University
New York, N.Y.

*NOTE: The MIT and Rutgers lectures, summarized in the original edition, were subsequently published in *Tradition*, 17:2, Spring 1978.

Acknowledgments

The Governing Board of HAMEVASER wishes to express its gratitude and thanks to all those who assisted us in preparation of this volume. We would like to thank all sources for the use of their material.

"Introduction," by Rabbi Aharon Lichtenstein. Adapted translation by Shalom Carmy from *Encyclopedia Hebraica*, Jerusalem, 1974, vol. 25, pp. 502–503. Translated with permission of the author.

"A Eulogy for R. Hayyim Heller," adapted translation by Shalom Carmy from *Shanah B'shanah*, Heichal Shlomo, Jerusalem, 5730 (1970), pp. 197–221.

"A Eulogy for the Talner Rebbe," prepared for publication by Rabbi Abraham R. Besdin with corrections and elaborations suggested by Rabbi Soloveitchik. This transcribed lecture originally appeared in the Boston *Advocate* on June 22, 1972. Reprinted with permission of Rabbi Abraham R. Besdin. [R.C.A. Second Series: No. 3)

"Jews at Prayer," adapted translation by Shalom Carmy with Menachem Kasdan from *Maayonot, Tefillah* 5724 (1964). Department of Torah Education for the Diaspora, pp. 9–11.

"*Sh'hora Ani V'nava*," adapted translation by David Martin from *Fir Drashot*, published by The Religious Zionists of America—Mizrachi—Hapoel Hamizrachi, 5727 (1967), pp. 11–14. The material translated here is the first section of a much larger Yiddish lecture entitled "The Ancestral Covenant."

"Torah and Humility," prepared by Joseph Adler.

"The First Rebellion against Torah Authority," based upon the prepared notes of Rabbi Abraham R. Besdin, R.C.A. Series of Prepared Rav Lecture Notes—Second Series: No. 1. Edited by Menachem Kasdan.

"*Aseret Hadibrot*," based upon *Divrei HaRav* and edited by Joel Wolowelsky. A similar and related lecture was given by Rabbi Soloveitchik at the R.C.A. convention of June 1970. A prepared summary of that *shiur* was printed in the R.C.A. Mah Nishmah Supplement Vol. 11 no. 4, June 1971, by Rabbi Abraham R. Besdin.

"The Covenantal Community," prepared by Nathan Kahan with Joseph Adler. This article is reprinted from HAMEVASER, Vol. XII, no. 4, December 20, 1973.

"The Unique Experience of Judaism," prepared by Menachem Kasdan. A similar and related article appeared in HAMEVASER, vol. XI, no. 1, May 23,1972.

"Adam and Eve," prepared by Marc Stern. This article was revised by the author from the original reconstruction as it appeared in HAMEVASER, vol. X, no. 4, January 1972.

"On the Nature of Man," prepared by Uri Levy. This article originally appeared in HAMEVASER, vol. I, no. 4, April 1971.

"The Role of The Judge," prepared by Joseph Adler.

"Two *T'shuva* Lectures," prepared by Mordecai Willig (5729) and Pinchas Weinberger (5734). The first article is reprinted from HAMEVASER vol. VII, no 2, October 1969 and the second article is reprinted with slight modifications from HAMEVASER vol. XII, no. 2, October 30, 1973 by Pinchas Weinberger.

"Insights into *M'gillat Esther*," prepared by Yaacov Tendler. This article originally appeared in HAMEVASER vol. XI, no. 6, May 8, 1973.

"Purim Ideas," prepared by Pinchas Weinberger. This article originally appeared in HAMEVASER Vol. XII, No. 5, March 13, 1974.

"On the Love of Torah: Impromptu Remarks at a *Siyyum*," prepared by Menachem Kasdan.

* * *

"Sacred and Profane" first appeared in *Hazedek*, May–June 1945, prepared for publication by Samuel Stollman; reprinted in *Gesher*, June 1966, with the help of Rabbi Aharon Lichtenstein.

"The Nine Aspects of the Haggada" appeared in *The Yeshiva University Haggada*, 1985, with notes by Rabbi Nathaniel Helfgot.

Introduction

Rabbi Joseph Dov Soloveitchik (b. 1903, Pruzhan), is one of the leading contemporary figures in halakha and Jewish thought, and a leader of Orthodox Judaism in the U.S. He is the grandson of R. Hayyim Soloveitchik. Until the age of twenty two he studied Torah from his father, R. Moshe, by whom he was profoundly influenced. In 1925, he entered the University of Berlin, where he studied philosophy, logic, and mathematics, receiving his doctorate for his dissertation on Hermann Cohen. In the same year he emigrated to the United States, where he became rabbi of the Orthodox Jewish community in Boston, where he still resides. Upon his father's death (1941), he succeeded him as Rosh Yeshivah at the Rabbi Isaac Elchanan Theological Seminary, in which role he educated a significant portion of the Orthodox rabbinate active today in the U.S. His influence over the Orthodox community was strengthened in 1952, when he assumed the chairmanship of the Halakhah Commission of the Rabbinical Council of America. His activity in the Religious Zionists of America—of which he served as honorary president—and his *d'rashot*, lectures, and *shiurim*, extended his influence. From 1950 on, he became the dominant spiritual personality within modern American Orthodoxy, urging involvement with the modern scene and a readiness to tackle the problems connected with this. His personality and background enabled him to maintain relationships and influence in rabbinic circles and yeshivot on the right, as well as among nontraditional elements on the left.

His talmudic methodology is principally based on that of his grandfather, R. Hayyim, although he broadened and polished it, modernized its terminology, and disseminated it within a larger community. It is, however, in the interaction of halakha and thought, that R. Soloveitchik has blazed a new and original trail. His basic assumptions are that the halakha is rooted in spiritual and ethical realities and that it is possible to construct a Jewish weltanschauung only on the basis of halakha in its completeness, through a thorough confrontation with all its spheres. The effort to clarify "the philosophy of halakha" finds, for him, varying expressions: concentration on matters of natural philosophical interest, such as the laws of prayer and festivals; lecture discourses in which the halakhic subjects and philosophical analysis are intertwined; lectures and essays on philosophical topics in the light of halakha. The subjects constituting the basic concepts of his thought are many and varied, some of them (such as freedom, holiness, and spiritual worship) highly abstract, but one of the most characteristic qualities of his discussions is precisely his relatedness to reality, his continual recourse to detail. Another characteristic is his dialectical use of different thought categories,such as *lamdut*, *ḥasidut* and Kabbalah, which he draws on heavily; and non-Jewish thought (Kierkegaard, K. Barth, R. Otto, E. Brunner), which has also influenced him.

His attitude toward the State of Israel also reflects a dialectical approach. He views the return to Zion and the establishment of the state as a historical process of tremendous importance; he stresses, however, a universal strand, according to which the basic shaping factors in the life of both the individual and the contemporary community are above any specific place: spiritual peaks are attainable in Exile as in Israel, and one should strongly oppose the "mythological" identification of *K'nesset Yisrael* with Israel to the neglect of the Diaspora existence past and present. The settlement of Israel is important as a mitzva among mitzvot and as a spur to religious-national renaissance—but, principally, it is an instrument and a means. The place is a factor—but the *Shekhina* can dwell in any place. One must give full-throated thanks for the existence of the State of Israel, but with the knowledge that it is only a step on the road to the realization of the prophetic, messianic, vision, as yet distant.

His teachings are mainly oral, and, following family tradition, he has yet to publish a book. Dozens of articles, nonetheless, have appeared on halakhic and theological subjects, the most famous of which are two long essays, "*Ish haHalakhah*" (*Talpiyot* 1, 5704) and "The Lonely Man of Faith" (*Tradition*, 7:2, Summer 1965).

Sacred and Profane: *Kodesh* and *Ḥol* in World Perspectives

1. Religion Versus Secularism

In the same fashion that *kodesh* and *ḥol* form the spiritual framework of our *halakha*, so do *kodesh* and *ḥol* determine the dichotomy of living experience into sacred and profane. This double classification of values and experience is not a Jewish one alone. The sacred and profane realms—religion and secularism —are cultural distinctions among peoples in all ages, from primitive animists to modern theologians.

Universal though this classification may be, this dualism has often been misapprehended. The *halakhic* conception of the essence of *ḥol* and *kodesh* is, as a matter of fact, diametrically opposed to universally the accepted formulation in the circles of religious liberalism, Jewish as well as non-Jewish.

For many religious world interpretations, secularism, as conceived theologically and empirically, is a state of uncertainty and fear, unrest and apprehension. It is a limitless, fathomless bourne in which man drifts and wanders as a straying, wind-tossed leaf. He finds no contentment or peace, no anchor or haven. He is the child of a jesting fate.

Religion, however, in contradistinction to mundane vulnerability, is a state of security and impregnability. It is a *festung* of peace and abiding hope, barricaded to the indifference of nature and the fluctuations of life. In this state man finds purpose and direction, an anchor and a haven. He becomes the child of a merciful Providence.

4

Such a view has shaped the general outlook of many pragmatic expositions of the essence of the religious act These behold in religion a refuge of repose for man, who is shattered by the numerous, discordant forces of the secular world; religion offers happiness and comfort. In such a spirit William James speaks of the "religion of the happy-minded" that serves him as a model of the religious attitude. It is no wonder that one of the most popular psalms in religious circles is "The Lord is my shepherd, I shall not want" [Psalms 23:1]. The idyllic canvas of green pastures and still waters upon which the Psalmist paints in quiet, soothing colors the gestalt of the God-worshipper harmonizes with the pragmatic analysis of the religious act, as one bringing man consolation and hope.

Man, upon entering the religious domain, unburdens himself of the many responsibilities and duties which press upon his mind, and he is relieved of the task of eternal vigilance and self-observation.

Perhaps such a philosophy is advantageous for the popularization of religious notions and ideas among the masses. It is easier to "sell" religion to the nonbeliever if you praise your merchandise as a transcendental "drug" or "opiate" conducive to the eradication of pain and misery. However, at the same time, it dispossesses the religious act of its zest and flavor, its multidimensionality and colorful content. It lures the religious act into the domain of *hedone*, to what Kierkegaard calls "technical wisdom."

The religious experience, however, is beyond granting man a hedonic status or spiritual complacency. To the contrary, the religious experience is fraught with pitfalls and continual challenge. God, if man finds Him, does not relieve the God-seeker of his imperatives but imposes new ones. Religion enriches life, gives it depth and multidimensional visions, but does not always grant man the comfort and complacency that nearly always spell superficiality and shallow-mindedness. The equation of a happy and concomitantly profound life is inadequate. The domain of sanctity is more intensely provocative and tortuous than the secular. The *homo religiosus* is wanting in mental balance and harmony to a greater degree than the mundane type. His mind seethes with antinomies and antithetic problems and questions that will never find their solution.

The error of modern representatives of religion is that they promise their congregants the solution to all the problems of life—an expectation that religion does not fulfill. Religion, on the contrary, deepens the problems but never intends to solve them. The grandeur of religion lies in its *mysterium tremendum*, its magnitude, and its ultimate incomprehensibility. To cite one example, we may adduce the problem of theodicy, the justification of evil in the world, which has tantalized the inquiring mind from time immemorial till this last tragic decade. The acuteness of this problem has grown for the religious person in essence and dimensions. When a minister, rabbi, or priest attempts to solve the ancient question of Job's suffering through a sermon or lecture, he does not promote religious ends but, on the contrary, does them a disservice. The beauty of religion, with its grandiose vistas, reveals itself to man not in solutions but in problems, not in harmony but in the constant conflict of diversified forces and trends. Unhampered by theological doctrine and dogma, the Greeks, in such an understanding, could freely divinate religious faith as "divine madness."

The ideal of Greek ethics was the harmonious personality; the balanced man, and the complete, proportionate nature. Aristotelian psychology and ethics derive from this ideal. Even as a physician, Aristotle analyzed sickness as disharmony and disturbance of proportion. However, the history of culture will attest, in many instances, that the creative geniuses of humanity have not always been harmonious personalities. Creation springs from primordial chaos; religious profundity springs from spiritual conflict. The Jewish ideal of the religious personality is not the harmonious individual determined by the principle of equilibrium, but the torn soul and the shattered spirit that oscillate between God and the world. In his substrata of spiritual experience, the *homo religiosus* endures constantly the diastrophic forces of mental upheaval and psychic collision.

Moses sees the burning bush. On the one hand, he covers his face in apprehension; he would escape the awesome sight. Yet, on the other hand, some mysterious, invisible force fascinates him and irresistibly draws him near. And he says to the great silence, "I will draw near and see this wondrous sight . . ." [Exodus 3:3].

This is not harmony and this is not the balanced attitude of the Stoic philosopher. It is, rather, the ideal of a personality torn between two powerful poles of fear and hope, dread and love. And is not the history of Israel a panorama of fluctuations, flight from God and then return? And the exodus from Egypt, the Revelation, the golden calf, the erection of the Temple, the episode of the spies, and later, in the age of the prophets, the constant alternation of serving God and deserting Him, do they not all symbolize heterogeneity and a chain of discrepancies rather than uniformity and homogeneity? It would appear that the supreme religious experience of Revelation did not suffice to grant full security and religious contentment to Israel; for they sinned while yet in the desert of Sinai, while yet in the shadow of the mount.

It is an empirical fact that *k'dusha* elevates man, not by vouchsafing him harmony and synthesis, balance and proportionate thinking, but by revealing to him the nonrationality and insolubility of the riddle of existence.

K'dusha is not a paradise but a paradox. The dangers involved in the realm of *k'dusha* are, by far, more hazardous than those predicated in the secular sphere.

This interpretation of *k'dusha* is reflected in the halakhic code. The halakha requires of man a more vigilant attitude in regards to *k'dusha* than to *ḥol*. Laws, like היסח הדעת, פיגול, נותר, יוצא, טומאה, and many others that affect only the sacred, not the profane, indicate the halakhic view that *k'dusha* can be easily corrupted. *K'dusha* intrinsicates *sh'mira*, continual and total awareness and diligence lest man fall from his high estate.

Moreover, religion, if corrupted through amoral applications, turns volte-face and becomes a negative, destructive force. When the golden calf was inscribed with the Ineffable Name, it became a negative force, not merely a neutralized force, wreaking havoc in the Jewish camp.

We have witnessed how the corruption of great ideals gave birth to evil forces in religious and ethical impregnation, more dangerous than evil fathered by evil. Love, the exalted concept of religion, was distorted into the persecution of heretics. The dignity of man, the lofty concept of the humanists, was transformed into the deification of man and the worship of the dictator. The spiritual concept of the state recrudesced into the fascist corporate state and to the consequent nothingness of the individual. *K'dusha* entails הורתה ולדתה בקדושה, the conception and fruition of a divine concept in the constant awareness of sanctity. The halakha is prescient to the fact that pitfalls are present in religious values. It presupposes that *k'dusha* involves both positive challenges and negative forces. It is aware that the struggle and challenge lie not in the seeking of religious values but in their keeping. This, then, is the halakhic conception of the states of *kodesh* and *ḥol*.

2. Place Consciousness

The two fundamental dimensions of *k'dusha* are מקום וזמן, "place consciousness" and "time consciousness." The halakhic violation of יוצא, נותר, חוץ לזמנו ומקומו are defections in place or in time. *K'dusha* may be profaned by such defections. What is this first dimension, the dimension of place consciousness?

It is an anthropological truism that man passed from a nomadic stage to a pastoral stage, and then from an agricultural stage to urbanization. From the functional standpoint, man has arrived at certain gains through this sociological evolution. The resident or settler has produced a more advanced culture than the nomad. Civilization is, primarily, the product of landed peoples. It was for this reason that Jeremiah urged the Rahabites, a nomadic tribe, to settle and prosper; for they had created nothing as a nomadic people.

In what ways is the settler who has his own "place" superior to the nomad who has none of his own? First, the nomad is an exploiter, a parasite. He moves from one pasture to another, from one feeding ground to another. When favorable ecological conditions turn, he lifts his tent and travels anew. He has neither the desire nor intent to cultivate his land, for he has no land of his own, and he can always find new pastures. Secondly, the nomad has no mental "bond" with his land. Since he has offered it nothing, it offers him nothing. He does not feel a symbiotic relationship between himself and his land. He has no "place consciousness."

The settler, however, is a producer and creator. This is his land; he tills and cultivates it. He prays for rain, and he combats the elements that would drive him from his land. He does not wish to find new pastures, for these are integrated with his existence. The settler has a land attachment. His land has become part and parcel of his mental set. He lives in a symbiotic relationship with his land. He has tilled it and it has produced. He loves it and merges in it. He has "place consciousness."

In the fratricide of Abel by Cain we figuratively observe the above contrast and its results: Cain was stronger than Abel because Cain was a farmer, a settler, while Abel was a shepherd, a nomad. Cain rose and slew his brother because he was the stronger; he had land attachments, and he fought for them. Abel, the nomad, was "weak" and knew not how to defend himself, for he had no "mental bonds" that would incite him to an act of defense. And the most fitting punishment for Cain was for him to become a nomad, wandering the earth, restless and derelict.

Nomads and settlers can be understood in a symbolic sense, in terms of spiritual values. Some people's relation to or appreciation of spiritual values and treasures resembles the relation of the nomad to his pastures, in both ways. First, he is a spiritual parasite; as long as nature feeds his flocks, he associates with his place, with certain values. But let his resources and wellsprings become exhausted and he lifts his tent and travels anew. Likewise do many appreciate values as long as they can enjoy them, as long as these values render satisfaction. This is the hedonic approach. As soon as an experience loses its value from the hedonic standpoint, it is deserted. Secondly, these people do not display any "place consciousness" in reference to spiritual norms and values. They are not fused with their ideals. They are not implanted in the deep strata of spirituality and sensate life, even when they enjoy and receive spiritual values. They have no world perspective of their own.

Early Jewish history passed through the phase of the nomad and into the phase of the settler. Our Sages have denoted this when they summarized the peregrinations of the *Shekhina* from Egypt to Palestine, from Shiloh which was called *ohel* [Psalms 78:60], symbol of the nomad, to the Temple, which was called *bayit* [II Samuel 7:5–7,13], symbol of the settler. The Jew did not attain full *k'dushat makom*, a sanctified place consciousness, until he settled on his land, in a true Jewish world perspective.

A world perspective is not a cognitive approach to the world; it is not merely a matter of knowledge. One may be acquainted with any culture although the object of one's knowledge need not be identical with one's personal outlook. Cognition does not make for a weltanschauung. The latter rests not on cognitive foundations but on a practical act of integration with the self. Knowledge, together with appreciation and valuation, comprises a world perspective. One must become integrated with his knowledge to call it his own. One must live symbiotically with his culture to make it a living experience. He must place himself in the "thickness" of his knowledge and experience it. World perspective is an all-enveloping "sensation" and a dynamic act of valuation. The modern theory of value, since Lotze, Windelband, and Rickert, the fathers of modern axiology, declares truth to be not a correlative to some ontological entity but a value that reigns supreme. If one says, "my culture," it implies not only the culture of "my acquaintance" but a culture which "I appreciate and value, love and admire, and finally even worship."

The modern exponents of *Weltanschauungslehre* see in philosophy not just a theoretical discipline but an intimate personal experience and worldview. They stress the personal relationship of the philosopher to his philosophy. (And this is the real meaning of philosophy, as derived from the Greek: love of wisdom.) In this point they demarcate between the scientist and the philosopher. The scientist is impartial; the philosopher is a passionate lover of his views.

Thus, the "spiritual nomad" is impartial, has cognition but no love for or integration with a culture. Thus, he is not "place conscious" in the sense of belonging to any particular culture or world perspective. In the settler, however, we observe the merger of the worshipper and his God, of the philosopher and his wisdom. One who has no such personal integration with a world perspective is a nomad. He has no place consciousness, no sense of "belongingness." He can have no *k'dusha.*

One may be acquainted with many cultures. Yet, the question is always pertinent: "What is my *makom,* my place? What is my world perspective?" For knowledge alone means nothing. The spiritual nomad may have universal knowledge and yet remain cultureless, for he does not experience his knowledge. It is only when knowledge becomes an integral part of his existence and consciousness, through the medium of mental bonds, that it may be truly said that the spiritual nomad has come home to a place of his own.

The tragedy of many modern Jews today lies in the fact that they are deserting an ancient heritage and, moreover, severing spiritual bonds with values which man admires or worships. They desert the realm of Jewish values but have not acquired new ones. Their tragedy lies not in their dearth of knowledge, for, quite to the contrary, modern Jews have much theoretical and practical knowledge; rather, it lies in the fact that they are lacking in the living experience of values, the passionate merger of the worshipper with the object of his worship. Indifferent knowledge and a skeptical approach to ideals and norms will never result in a multidimensional personality. The modern Jew is a spiritual wanderer, and this spiritual wanderer includes not only the nonpious Jew but even a certain type of observant Jew, for piety which is not based on Torah and knowledge does not constitute the ideal of Jewish religiosity.

The religious telos finds its full realization in the passionate religious life, permeated with enthusiasm and rapture, which opens to man new vistas and enchanted horizons. Religious inspiration awakens a vision of God as the frame and space of the world. "I live in God; I think, feel, and exist through Him; He permeates my life and gives it meaning and content." The dualism that is so prevalent in other religions, namely, the division of a profane and sacred domain, is transcended. The entire universe is converted into one monistic realm, the domain of God. Street and home, the synagogue and the shop, merge. The whole of man's life becomes dedicated to God.

Thus, the Jews gave God the remarkable attribute of *makom*, place. The Lord is envisaged as the *M'komo shel olam*, the repository of the universe. What is this attribute of "place" for a God Who is infinite and omnipresent? By intuiting the attribute of *makom*, the halakha revealed to the world a revolutionary concept of God. He is not transcendent, mysterious, and inapproachable, but our immediate Companion. We live in God and experience Him in His full immediacy. As the settler experiences his home, as man intuits space, so does the Jew intuit God. He does not arrive at Him through philosophical speculation or metaphysical inference, but he meets Him through experience and intuition. הקדוש ברוך הוא, הוא מקומו של עולם, ואין העולם מקומו , God is the repository of the universe. All is contained in Him. He does not repose in me; He is not just one phase of my world perspective; He envelops all. If the universe is unthinkable without a space frame (and this is, indeed, the crux of Kant's a priori concept), so much more so is the Jewish world incomprehensible without an all-embracing God.

It is these two elements, cognition and integration, that make for a world perspective and, for the Jew, a *k'dushat makom*. Without the idea of place consciousness, the state of *k'dusha*, sanctity, can never be acquired or held. For the approach to God is only through the application of place consciousness. When one implants himself in the cultural sphere of the Torah and merges with its intrinsic trends, he may claim that he has found God. Without the all-enveloping and all-inclusive space intuition, the ideation of divinity is almost impossible. Even the atheist experiences, at times, the mysterious feeling of the pantheist, of being enveloped by God.

ובשר בשדה טרפה לא תאכלו [Exodus 22:30]. The definition of *t'reifa* was given by the Sages as any object that transcends its own boundaries. Such a one is a torn body, a soul bereft of place. The Jewish attitude denies self-transcendence of *k'dusha*. It requires of holiness to be space- and boundary-conscious. Place consciousness is a basic condition for the realization of the *k'dusha* ideal.

3. Time Consciousness

The other dimension or principle of *k'dusha* is *z'man*, "time consciousness." Bergson's tremendous influence upon modern philosophy is partly due to the fact that he formulated a new interpretation of time, the so-called pure "durée," duration. He contrasted this concept of time with that of the physicist, which is pure chronometry, time quantified and frozen in geometric space, time associated with space in motion and, in modern physics, with the time-space continuum.

Thus, Bergson speaks of fleeting time, living and immeasurable, beyond the scientist's mesh. No clock can be applied to this qualitative time, which is transient, intangible, and evanescent, and, on the other hand, creative, dynamic, and self-emerging. In this "time" there are no milestones separating past, present, and future. It is not unidimensional, as is physical time, but multidimensional, compenetrating and overlapping past, present, and future.

With this qualitative time, Bergson contrasts quantitative time. This is time measured by the clock, by the rotation of the Earth on its axis, and by its revolution about the sun. This "time" is uniform, empty and noncreative.

While Bergson limited himself to a philosophical and metaphysical analysis of time, we may proceed further and posit this dualistic time concept as the prime norm of human life that carries with it practical implications and ethical aspects. Man encounters the alternative of molding time in a quantitative or qualitative pattern.

There are some people who live in quantitative, dead time. They measure time by the clock and by the calendar. For them there is no merger of the past and the future. The present itself is a lost moment. A year is endless. How much more so centuries and tens of centuries! These people are deprived of an historical consciousness; for history is the living experience of time.

The man, however, who lives in qualitative time has a different criterion of the experience of time than the quantitative experience. He measures time not by length-extensio but by pure quality, creativity, and accomplishment. While for the man with a quantitative apprehension all fractions of time are equal because all represent physical "t's"; for the man of qualitative apprehension, there is no equality among temporal fractions of time. Moments are heterogeneous. One may live an entire lifespan quantitatively, not having lived even a moment qualitatively. And, contrariwise, one may have lived a moment quantitatively and have lived through an eternity qualitatively. The alternative is up to man himself. The time norm is the highest criterion by which man, life, and actions should be judged.

Oriental history has given us the best example of such an alternative. Oriental culture and technology is much older than that of Europe or America. Yet qualitatively America is—as regards technology certainly—older than China, for America has created more in one hundred fifty years than China in five thousand. History is concerned not with quantity but with accomplishment. History ultimately is not a composite of calendar time but a qualitative living entity. Wherein did the Orient fail until recently in keeping "time" with the Occident? There is one answer: in the differing time consciousness of these two civilizations. China apprehended time as a fact while America envisaged it as a norm.

Those historians who fell in love with the Orient for its Stoic calmness and indifference to the passage of time and who felt the breath of eternity there have misapprehended time and eternity. Eternity is to be conceived not in quantitative uniformity but in qualitative creativity and mutability.

What is true for entire cultures is equally true for individual personalities. There are some people who are always "time thirsty." There are others, however, who are "time-saturated." One who fathoms the spirit of time becomes a *yotzer olamot*, a creative personality. The problem of the creative personality today is one of time; it is too short. The finite character of time is one of the most crying tragedies of men's life. Yet, if a man lives by quantitative measurements, the problem of time is reversed; he is surfeited by it.

The individual who measures time in purely quantitative terms is an essentially passive personality. He is a recipient and not a giver, a creature rather than a creator. His prototype is the slave. The slave has no time consciousness of his own, for he has no time of his own. The awareness of הזמן גרמא, the full intuition of the qualitative moment, is alien to him. Absolved by homogenous, changeable time, he lacks affinity for a duty whose execution depends solely on time, on a "now" and "not later"; upon a "today" and "not tomorrow," upon a night whose dawn cancels the opportunity, upon a day whose sunset eliminates the possibility. He does not understand the full impact of such dicta as "אם לא עכשיו אימתי?" ("If not now, then when?") [*Avot* 1:14] and "אם שיחקה לך השעה אל תחמיתנה" ("If the hour beckons, do not delay").

The basic criterion which distinguishes freeman from slave is the kind of relationship each has with time and its experience. Bondage is identical with passive intuition and reception of an empty, formal time stream.

When the Jews were delivered from the Egyptian oppression and Moses rose to undertake the almost impossible task of metamorphosing a tribe of slaves into a "nation of priests" [Exodus 19:16], he was told by God that the path leading from the holiday of Pesaḥ to Shavu'ot, from initial liberation to consummate freedom (*Gillui Shekhina*, Revelation), leads through the medium of time. The commandment of *s'fira* was entrusted the Jew; the wondrous test of counting forty-nine successive days was put to him. These forty-nine days must be whole. If one day be missed, the act of numeration is invalidated.

A slave who is capable of appreciating each day, of grasping its meaning and worth, of weaving every thread of time into a glorious fabric, quantitatively stretching over the period of seven weeks but qualitatively forming the warp and woof of centuries of change, is eligible for Torah. He has achieved freedom.

We may say then that qualitative-time consciousness is comprised of two elements: First, the appreciation of the enormous implications inherent in the fleeting moments of the present. No fraction of time, however infinite, should slip through the fingers, left unexploited; for eternity may depend upon the brief moment. Secondly, the vicarious experience, while in the present, of the past and future. No

distance, however removed, should separate one's time
consciousness from the dawn of one's group or from the
eschatological destiny and infinite realization of one's
cherished ideals.

האב זוכה לבן בנוי, בכח ובעושר ובחכמה ובשנים ובמספר הדורות
לפניו והוא הקץ שנאמר: קורא הדורות מראש אע"פ שנאמר ועבדום
ועינו אותם ארבע מאות שנה ונאמר ודור רביעי ישיבו הנה.

Rabbi Akiva said, "The father endows the son with his
beauty, strength, means, wisdom, years, and the number
of generations to come. And this is the *Ketz,* the Redemption;
as it is written, '. . . they shall enslave them and afflict
them four hundred years' [Genesis 15:13]; and it is written,
'And in the fourth generation they shall return here . . .'
[ibid. 15:16]" (*Eduyot* 3a).

How are we to interpret this comment of the Mishna? The
various commentators of the Talmud have found it obscure.
Let us attempt to resolve this mishna in the light of what we
have said.

We may conjecture that Rabbi Akiva delivered such a
message in the chaotic, strife-torn days of his time. Israel
tottered precariously on the brink of the tentative explosion
of Bar Kokba's revolt, which Rabbi Akiva had prophesied
and urged so zealously: דרך כוכב מיעקב. "A star hath flared
forth from Jacob" [Numbers 24:17] that would illumine the
dark days of Israel whose sun had been eclipsed by the
rising might of Rome. In that abysmal period there were
many who counseled moderation and self-control. They
pointed at the immature character of such a rebellion, that
the time had not yet come to take arms against the might of
Rome. In effect, the revolutionists were ranged against the
"evolutionists." The old problem of whether man should
interfere with the historic process or paths of "fate" in actively
determining the course of the same had come to a head. It

was a time to accept or reject a policy of laissez faire toward history. It was a time for meeting and confuting the objections of the moderators who warned of the immaturity and jeopardy of a Bar Kokhba. And in countering their cries of a hands-akimbo policy to the historic process, Rabbi Akiva delivered this grand view of the twofold approach to time, *minyan ha-shanim—mispar ha-doroth.*

It is undoubtedly true, if time is measured quantitatively by the מנין השנים that only seventy years separate the Bar Kokhba revolt from the destruction of the Temple, and it is too short a period to bring about a national renaissance and prepare a nation for political autonomy. But, if time is measured qualitatively, by the מספר הדורות, what the "generations" accomplish in time, if time be measured not by the clock but by the creativity of a nation, then, in seventy years, a nation may condense an epoch, an eternity, and even become worthy of liberty and autonomy. If the past is alive, אב זוכה לבן "the father endows the son" [*Eduyot* 3a], then the future is already born.

As a divine proof, Rabbi Akiva quoted two contradictory decrees as to the duration of the Egyptian bondage. One decree involved four centuries, the other, four generations, considerably less. This, in effect, is the substance of Rabbi Eliezer's reconciliation of the apparent contradiction of the two decrees. In *Pirkei d'Rabbi Eliezer* he offers the explanation of "merit," כאן שזכו וכאן שלא זכו. The alternatives of the decrees are resolved in terms of time consciousness. If the Jew is "meritorious," worthy of and alert to the qualitative creative consciousness of time, the decree extends the exile to the fourth generation. However, if the Jew has not attained this kind of time intuition but measures time by quantification, the Egyptian exile will extend to a fourth century. The two decrees denote not irrational divine judgments but an evolutionary cycle of metamorphosis.

The children of Abraham, who had brought the message
of liberty to the peoples of the world, had to pass through
two transitory periods: from freemen into an oppressed
people, and, again, from a man-swarm of slaves and
bondsmen into a chosen people. Their metamorphosis from
a slave people and a slave mentality into a free people and
"nation of priests" [Exodus 19:6] prepared to witness the
greatest miracle of all time—the Revelation—was a problem
of evolution.

Should the Jew develop the qualitative consciousness of
time, his transitional period would expire in four generations.
With a qualitative consciousness of time, he could create a
prophet, a Moses, in four generations. But if he measured
time quantitatively, by the sands of time sweeping endlessly
over the pyramids of the Pharaohs, then even four hundred
years would be too little. Then he would share with the
Sphinx the unchanged scene of the Egyptian desert. Then
would the Lord apply His own criterion of time: "For a
thousand years in Your sight are as a yesterday . . ." [Psalms
90:4].

The ideal of *Ketz*, of the "end of the road," can never be
realized if it be sought after in quantitative terms; then the
process is snail-paced and the stages demarcated by infinite
coulisses of time. The process would be akin to the paradox
of Zeno, of the tortoise pursuing Achilles. If time be
quantitative, a unidimensional composite of discrete,
infinitesimal moments, then the tortoise will never overtake
Achilles, and the Jew will never attain salvation.

Ketz, Redemption, is not something static and distant toward
which man gravitates, for as such it would be only an
ever-regressing mirage in the deserts of time; rather, it is an
ideal or norm which man himself quickens into life. Only
by qualitative criteria of norms and creativity can man shorten
the distance and span time with great leaps. Modern

technology has conquered space. *It is the ideal of* Ketz *to conquer time.*

And this was, in effect, the revolutionary message of Rabbi Akiva, who urged his people to revolt against the Romans. The concept of a slow historical process that was so popular among the peoples who lived under the influence of Greek philosophy, the endless morphological evolution from matter into form, from a lower to a higher eidetic stage, carries weight and significance so far as time is lived through quantitatively. Then the forces of history move with an extremely slow pace; years, decades, and centuries are nothing but drops in the sea of eternity. What does a century mean in geological evolution? A nation, not comprehending the Janus face of time or the alternatives that time proffers, may be subject to the same laws and regulations of the cosmic process in nature. Under the aspect of מנין השנים, "quantitative years," any rebellion is a priori doomed to a stillbirth. If man leaves his fate to the principle of blind, mechanical causality and circumstantial determination, he can never attain salvation and redemption. *Ketz* is nonexistent for him as chaos and confusion are precluded in the realm of nature.

The Jews have inherited from Abraham the alternative to מנין השנים. The prophecy of the "generations" challenges man not to live in time but to mold it, to give to the indifferent chronos new aspects and a new interpretation. Time is computed according to man's own creativity and self-determination. All laws of immutable and unalterable causality fail if man participates in the mysterious unfolding of the chronos. A qualitative time experience enables a nation to span a distance of hundreds and thousands of years in but a few moments. To consider time from the aspect of מספר הדורות, of the "generations" which live in it, entails the mystery of *Ketz—Ge'ula.*

If the idea of a Bar Kokhba revolt is not ripe, continued

Rabbi Akiva, then we can never achieve the realization of
Ketz. If *Ketz* is possible, then quantitative measurements of
time are irrelevant and nonexistent. In the seventy years
from the destruction of the Temple until the outbreak of the
Bar Kokhba upheaval, the Jewish people may have lived
through an endless continuum of time, he concluded. "והוא
הקץ." And then will be your Redemption!

Stefan Zweig writes of this same time velocity that
accelerated his event-filled life. In *World of Yesterday* he
relates what is, in effect, a contrast of quantitative time with
qualitative time:

> My father, my grandfather, what did they see? Each
> of them lived his life in uniformity. A single life from
> beginning to end, without ascent, without decline,
> without disturbance or danger, a life of slight anxieties,
> hardly noticeable transitions. In even rhythm, leisurely
> and quietly, the wave of time bore them from the
> cradle to the grave.
>
> But in our lives there was no repetition; nothing of
> the past survived, nothing came back. It was reserved
> for us to participate to the full in that which history
> formerly distributed, sparingly and from time to time,
> to a single country, to a single century (ibid., 3rd ed.
> [London: Cassell and Co. Ltd., 1944], pp. 6–7).

For the man of the street ancient history is something dim
and distant, viewed in the *dämmerung* of the mythological
coulisses of time.

The man of the street has no personal relationship with,
no consciousness of continuity and interdependency between
the glorious periods of antiquity and the emerging present.
Even medieval and modern history, from which not many
years separate us, appears mythical, romantic, and elusive—a
refuge for escapists.

But the Jew of the *masora* has a different conception of
time. Revelation and tradition erase the bounds of time.

Distance in time is nonexistent for him. Thousands of years may have elapsed but he walks back and forth from antiquity to modern times. The chief success of the old *ḥeder*, though deficient in many respects, lay in this spirit of compenetration of a distant past and a dim future with an immediate present.

For Jewish boys and girls, Abraham is not a mythical figure but an ever-present inspiration. They live through his tribulations and wanderings. They travel with him from Syria to Palestine. They feel the fear and trembling of Isaac on the *akeda*. They escape with Jacob to Ḥaran. They are imprisoned with Joseph in the pit. They rejoice in his ascendancy to high office and fame. They lead the Jews with Moses in the desert of Sinai. They sing with David. They are exalted with the prophets. They laugh with Rabbi Akiva. They meditate with Rambam. These figures are not dead or historical "have-beens" for the children of the *ḥeder* or the adults of the halakha, but dynamic, living heroes who visit the Jew from time to time, bringing him comfort, inspiration, and hope.

כל בי שמשי הוה אתי [רבי] לביתיה (כתובות ק"ג.). In moments of mental elevation, of spiritual exaltation, in times of *k'dusha*, the figure of Rebbi would appear to the Jews.

Upon this phenomenon of an historical continuum was founded the strength of *masora*, conceived as an historic stream of Jewish spirit whose tributaries of past, present, and future merged in each other. This is real historical consciousness. This is qualitative consciousness. Quantitative time creates but archeological consciousness of periods gone by that do not infiltrate into one's own ego existence.

When the Jew, on the holy day of Yom Kippur, sought to symbolize the contrast between the temporality of the moment and time as one living, creative stream, and the consequences of each, he prepared two sacrifices, שעיר לה' ושעיר לעזאזל. The kid consecrated to God was confined to one environ, the

עזרה, the courtyard of the Temple. If the kid were sacrificed outside its appointed place, it would become שחוטי חוץ, a profaned offering. The שעיר לעזאזל, the kid condemned to the wastes of the desert, however, became a wanderer, with no appointed place. The one entrusted with the Temple offering, the שעיר לה׳, was the high priest, the representative of tradition, time, and eternity, of *masora* and *y'rusha*. The one who led the שעיר לעזאזל into the desert was the איש עתי [Leviticus 16:21], the "man of the moment."

Thus, there were two distinctions between the two "kids." The שעיר לה׳ was under the aegis of the high priest, symbol of eternity and qualitative time consciousness, and also confined to the עזרה, symbol of קדושת מקום, place consciousness. On the other hand, the שעיר לעזאזל was under the supervision of the איש עתי, symbol of temporality and quantitative consciousness, confined to no place and welcome to none. These two were contrasted with each other in terms of both time consciousness and place consciousness. Place and time went hand in hand.

And what did this *ish itti* do to sustain himself while following the homeless scapegoat? He stopped at the "ten booths" (*Yoma* 66b) set up on the way from Yerushalayim to Tzuk, the Sages tell us. In each *sukka* was placed water and food. The time-unconscious man wanders from one resting place to another, seeking sustenance for the moment. He has neither place consciousness nor time consciousness. He is a "spiritual nomad." He has no culture, religion, or philosophical outlook of his own.

Thus, in this rite, the Jew depicted the true halakhic world perspective of place and time consciousness. Only the שעיר לה׳, who had both, was a fitting consecration to God. The other became a nomad with no past, present, or future. He had no other fate but the wastelands.

The timeless wanderer has no שדה אחוזה [Leviticus 26:16]

or קברות אבותי [II Chronicles 35:24]. He cannot say קדשה לשעתה וקדשה לעתיד לבוא [M'gilla 10a]. For him there is no place merger—God's Chosen House, which leads to time consciousness and eternity. בית הבחירה is synonymous with בית עולמים. The Chosen House is the Eternal House.

4. Creative T'shuva

Tonight, on the yahrzeit of my father, R. Moses Soloveitchik, it seems to me as if my father were yet alive, although four years have come and gone since his death. It is in a qualitative sense that I experience his nearness and spirit tonight. I cannot explain the דמות דיוקנה של אביו [Sota 36b], the spiritual picture of father that hovers near me tonight as in a yesteryear of physical existence.

Our Sages have said, גדולים צדיקים במיתתן יובר מבחייהן—"The righteous are exalted in death more than in life" [Ḥullin 7b]. If time be measured qualitatively, we may understand how their influence lingers on after their death and why the past is eternally bound with the present. Yet, how do their mortal lives acquire a new significance in death?

Qualitative time awareness reduces, in effect, to interspersing the text of chronology with values and creativity. These values appear in their true perspective when the stream of time undulates them away to the shores of yesterday. From the vantage point of the present, we first evaluate the significance of the past. When we are no longer at one with our values, we first begin to appreciate, evaluate, and even worship them. It is through this effect of contrast that we first arrive at qualitative time consciousness, a multidimensional continuum of past, present, and future. It is through contrast that quantitative time must have a stop and qualitative time a renewed impetus. And so is it with persons or values. When they have disappeared from the stage of the present, they take on a new and profound significance in contrast with the changed scene. Then the hills become smaller and the mountains larger, as time and perspective recede.

There is a concept dating from Plato that the basic values of man's personality (taken in a broad sense) are not fully evaluated in his lifetime or while he has them. An example of this concept is health. While one is imbued with the euphoria of health he is not keenly aware of his physical state. He fails to appreciate the treasure of health. It is only when one has first become ill that he first realizes what health means.

In his pessimistic temperament Schopenhauer contended that we understand health through sickness, pleasure through pain, and good through evil. This awareness through contrast is also apparent in the concept of home or fatherland. We have the striking example today in the sentiments of soldiers overseas. Many had to leave America to first discover it. In the byways of New Guinea Americans first pined for the thoroughfares of Main Street. In the vastness of the Pacific, sailors longed for their country lakes and streams. Americans first begin to evaluate their fabulous prewar living standard in the strictures of war economy. Men pine for peace in time of war.

What is it that breeds complacency in man to his vital values while he has them? Because these values form such an integral part of his physical and mental makeup, they become identical with his psyche, and he, therefore, loses the perspective that only an Archimedean point of distance and contrast may give him. Man is most shortsighted when he would view his own psyche. Man walking the circular Earth sees only a plain.

It is in this light that our Sages envisaged the great man's role. His inspiration may flourish on after his death for those with a qualitative appreciation of time and history.

And this concept of contrast carries weight not only in a mundane sense of health and home, and also for certain religious values, but also for the highest value in man's life—awareness of God. God from afar fascinates one more than God in one's immediacy. The modern Jew has first understood the prophet's cry, "מרחוק ה׳ נראה לי" [Jeremiah 31:2]. It is today that "God appears to me from afar . . . ." Many a time in our history we did not appreciate the nearness of God or His significance as much as we do today, when in many respects we are so distant from Him.

It is this same concept of contrast, of first becoming aware of the Lord "from afar," that is intrinsicated in *t'shuva*—repentance. The traditional view is that the *t'shuva* idea is penitence. For the Christian theologian, *t'shuva* is a transcendent act dependent upon the grace of God, Who is all-merciful and benevolent. The erasure of man's sins is, from the rational standpoint, incomprehensible. Only the supernatural, miraculous intercession of God on behalf of the sinner may effectuate this cleansing. The task of the sinner is to repent, to mortify himself, to practice castigation, to cry and implore for divine mercy and pity. The convert, according to this concept, is a passive, pitiful creature who begs for and attends divine grace.

The halakhic interpretation of *t'shuva* differentiates between penitence and purification—*kappara* (catharsis) and *tahara*. *Kappara*, penitence and absolution, is similar, in effect, to the universal concept of conversion, in toto. It is not a psychological phenomenon but a theological one, transcendent and nonrational. To alter the past is an act which denies the laws of causality and regulation in men's life.

But the halakhic concept of *t'shuva* contains yet another element: *tahara*, purification. This concept is one that predicates not the removal of sin but its exploitation. The *tahara* idea is, rather, to change the vectorial force of sin, its direction and destination. When the sinner of the first category attempts to forget his sin and beseeches God to erase it, the Jewish repentant strives to "remember" his sin, וחטאתי נגדי תמיד [Psalms 51:5] . He strives to convert his sin into a spiritual springboard for increased inspiration and evaluation. This act is not supernatural but psychological. It conveys one law in mental causality; although a cause is given, the effect need not equal the cause. The effect need not be predetermined. Man himself may determine the vectorial character of the effect and give it direction and destination.

In the biographies of great men we frequently encounter the fact that certain personages rose to tremendous heights because of a prior rapid descent. They transposed misdeeds into springboards of a heroic life and lofty ideas. Great nations possess the same ability. In a time of cultural decadence and mental disintegration, historical errors may, if the proper spirit of renaissance captures the national conscience, be transformed into a driving force which gravitates toward the finest and best in human life. National renaissance rises phoenixlike from the ashes of cultural dissolution. Ascent presupposes descent, ירידה צורך עלייה.

This faculty can best be understood in the light of "contrast." Sin reveals to man the beauty of good. Crime reveals the glory of the ethical. Mental disintegration reveals the enchantment of spiritual perfection. Values lost are more fascinating than ideals which are fully realized. The halakhic concept of *t'shuva* vouchsafes us the revelation that there are new values accessible to man from the springboard of sin and that in attaining them the spirit of man can, and does, not only conquer sin but exploit it as a constructive, creative force.

Tahara does not entail the act of reinstating man into a

former status of repeating the past, in copying previous good deeds and performances. It must not only activate one to return to a former status of innocence and righteousness (for then the contamination itself would serve no purpose or telos but would be superfluous) but must also convert and elevate one to a new stage. It must energize an ever-ascending spiral in man's spiritual state.

ה׳ ה׳ אני ה׳ קודם שיחטא ואני ה׳ אחר שיחטא; "I am the Lord before man sins, and I am the Lord after man sins" (*Rosh Hashana* 17b). But man's comprehension and awareness of the Lord after the sin is much superior to the idea of God that he cultivated in his purity and innocence.

> אמר ר׳ עקיבה אשריכם ישראל לפני מי אתם מטהרין מי מטהר
> אתכם אביכם שבשמים שנאמר וזרקתי עליכם מים טהורים וטהרתם
> ואומר מקוה ישראל ה׳ מה מקוה מטהר את הטמאים אף הקב״ה
> מטהר את ישראל׳

> Said Rabbi Akiva: Fortunate are you, Israel! Before Whom do you purify yourselves? Who purifies you? Your Father in Heaven. As it is said, "I will sprinkle pure water upon you; you shall be pure . . ." (Ezekiel 36:25). And it says, "God is the *mikve* of Israel . . ." (Jeremiah 17:13)—Just as a *mikve* punfies the impure, the Holy One Blessed Be He purifies Israel (*Yoma* 85b).

In Jabneh, the first Yom Kippur in exile, the Jews were left without the Temple and its ceremonial rites requisite for atonement, *kappara.* The Jewish community was perplexed and disconsolate. They could not imagine that the beautiful ideals incarnated in the symbols of the day could be realized and effectuated without the performance of the high priest, without the ceremonial of the two kids, without the ceremony in the Holy of Holies, and without the public confession and sacrifices. They could not see how to dispense with all the glory and pomp which used to be displayed in the

Temple on the day of atonement. The act of *t'shuva* and
kappara was closely associated in their minds with all these
external and ceremonial acts. How can a Jew attain absolution
and dispensation before God without the intercession and
worship forms of the high priest? It seemed as if, in the
smoke of the destroyed Temple, the Jewish vision of *t'shuva*
and Yom Kippur had also disappeared.

Then rose Rabbi Akiva, the majestic מצחק, the unswerving
"optimist," and he said: There is no need for such mournfulness
and helplessness. Indeed, we have been bereft of the Temple
and its divine dispensation of grace for the atonement of
sin. But we have lost only *kappara*, atonement and penitence,
but not *tahara*, purification. Besides *kappara* we still possess
a lofty idea, far superior to absolution. Indeed, we have
been bereft of the ceremonies and sacrifices that are relevant
to the transcendent act of the erasure of sin by supernatural
grace and incomprehensible divine benevolence that alter
the past and disrupt the causal chain. The attainment of
kappara will not be as complete and perfect now as it was
when the cult worship acts of the high priest brought man
into contact with transcendent and incomprehensible divinity.
But we Jews have brought another message of *t'shuva* to
man, that of *tahara*. There is nothing transcendent,
miraculous, or nonrational about *tahara*. It rests not without
but within causality. It is the discovery of a causal principle
in spiritual and mental life—that the conflict created in a
negative A may give birth to a positive B, by the rule of
contrast.

The act of *tahara*, in which sin is not eradicated but, on
the contrary, becomes part of my ego and is arrested and
retained in its negative emergence and corruptive powers,
awakens a creative force that shapes a new and loftier
personality. There is no place here for worship or sacrifices.
The performance of *tahara* is not directed at a transcendent

divinity but at God, as our Father, Companion, and intimate Counselor Who does not require any mysterious cult ceremonies or sacrifices. This *tahara* is based on an intimate relationship between man and God, creature and Creator, son and Father. And this communion of God and man has not been affected by the loss of outward ceremonial rites. לפני מי אתם מטהרים, לפני אביכם שבשמים [ibid.].

This natural concept of conversion which is not dissimilar to the unfolding process of mental life has not vanished with the disappearance of the Temple. On the contrary, it now has enhanced meaning and content. שנאמר מקוה ישראל ה' [ibid.]. The word "*mikve*," in its literal translation, signifies hope. God is the "hope of Israel." But Rabbi Akiva associated another meaning with "*mikveh*," that of purification symbolized by a water reservoir. And indeed, hope and purification are synonymous. When man stumbles and falls, becomes contaminated with sin, he should not despair or resign himself; but he should cultivate hope, not only for regaining but for "gaining" by his experience new visions and vistas. *Mikveh* is both hope and purification. Purification is nothing more than the anticipation of a more glorious future. Our ideal is not repetition but recreation on a higher level. And כך הקב"ה מטהר אב ישראל. *T'shuva* contains hope and *tahara*. Such an idea of *t'shuva* is not limited to any Temple or act of worship. All one requires is "before God," striving toward.

Growth from Afar

The concept of contrast and growth must serve as a practical preachment for the rabbinate today. Many rabbis have confided to me that the secular world they enter, once having left the environs of the yeshiva, jolts their values and threatens their ideology. This reorientation to new environments has become gradually one of the major problems of the young rabbi. But it is just this contrast that can serve as the true perspective for one's traditional values, not alone to regain and reaffirm former comprehension and intuition but to vouchsafe a new focus and enhanced endearment of values. It is only through this contrast of values with values, profane with sacred, that one may begin to grow in fortitude and self-realization. The secular world may serve even more than the religious to foster new concepts and overtones in the old. It must be understood that true consciousness of *k'dusha* comes in the dissatisfaction with the secular world, through the principal of contrast. It is ever and anon the prophet's revelation, "God appears to me from afar . . ." [Jeremiah 31:2]. And the Lord from afar is dearer and more intriguing than the Lord from near.

In concluding this yahrzeit address, I recall the midrash of the Sages:

> Before a man departs this world the Lord sends the angels to his sojournment to discover what men have to say of him. As soon as the man dies, he immediately enters his heavenly home. [*Midrash Kohelet* 12:13]

While a man lives, we must question ourselves in a positive effort to discover what he means to us, for we are all too unaware of the significance of what we enjoy. However, once the man dies, "he immediately enters his heavenly home." Once a personage has vanished from our lives, then the niche he filled stands starkly empty before us. We need no longer make an effort to understand him in his full significance. It becomes revealed to us in a great effulgence of light. מטתו פורחת באויר [ibid.]. Then his gestalt hovers in the higher spheres.

The Nine Aspects of the Haggada

The Haggada is based upon and revolves around the section in the Torah known as the "*Arami oved avi*" portion, which appears at the beginning of *Sidrat Ki Tavo* (Deuteronomy 26).[1] This is the passage that each Jew recited upon bringing the first fruits, the *bikkurim,* to the Temple in Jerusalem. It is clear from the Talmud in *Pesaḥim,*[2] and Rambam's codification in *Hilkhot Ḥametz u-Matza,*[3] that the recitation of this passage is essential to the fulfillment of the mitzva of *sippur y'tziat Mitzrayim.* Why in fact do our sages choose this passage as the focal point of the Haggada?[4]

We must conclude that each Jew, in addition to offering the first fruits, was commanded to fulfill the mitzva of *sippur y'tziat Mitzrayim.* Thus there are two times during the year that the Jew must relate the story of the exodus from Egypt; at the *hava'at bikkurim* and on the night of the Seder.

The Torah presented us with the text for the *hava'at bikkurim.* However, with regard to the Seder night all that we find in the Torah is the general commandment: "You shall tell your son on that day, saying, this is done (the *Pesaḥ* observance) because of what the Eternal did for me when I came out of Egypt" (Exodus 13:8).[5] A specific text is not mandated. *Ḥazal,* however, concluded that the "*Arami oved avi*" text which fulfilled the requirement of *sippur* at the bringing of the *bikkurim,* would also be appropriate at the Seder.

The use of a common text indicates that the seemingly distinct rituals, in fact, have a common theme or purpose. That purpose is to give thanks and express gratitude to the Almighty. Both recitations are acts of *hakkarat ha-tov* to the Eternal.

The essence of the Seder, and hence that of *sippur y'tziat Mitzrayim*, is the expression of gratitude to the Almighty on the great liberation and miracles that he wrought for us in Egypt. As Rambam states in *Sefer ha-Mitzvot*: "We are commanded to tell the story at the beginning of the fifteenth of Nisan. . . and we are to thank Him for all the goodness He has bestowed upon us" (*Mitzva* 157)[6] On the Seder night at the climax of *Maggid* we say: "Therefore we are obligated to thank and praise . . . exalt and revere Him who performed all those miracles and for us."[7]

Similarly, the act of *hava'at bikkurim* is an expression of thanksgiving and gratitude to the Almighty for granting the farmer and the people this holy land and its abundance after a history of wandering and suffering.[8] The Jew recognizes that this land has come to him and his nation through a chain of miraculous and divinely ordained episodes throughout history. Therefore, the *Arami oved avi* passage contains a short synopsis of early history, with an emphasis on the enslavement in Egypt, the Exodus and the entry into the Land of Israel. The Jew, when bringing the *bikkurim* states: "I say today before the Lord, your God . . ."[9] However, the Targum of Yonatan Ben Uziel translates: "I will give gratitude and praise this day to the Lord . . ."[10] The passage was understood by *Hazal* as a statement of thanksgiving and gratitude to the Almighty. (In fact, from this comment of the Targum it is possible to suggest that the word Haggada does not only imply the idea of "telling," but also the notion of thanksgiving and gratitude.)

1) Let us now analyze some of the various aspects of the Haggada. It will help us to begin with a comparison of the *sippur y'tziat Mitzrayim* that the Jew engages in at the *hava'at ha-bikkurim* and that of the Seder night. The common feature and first aspect of *sippur y'tziat Mitzrayim* on both these occasions is the *sippur*. We read and tell a story. This

recitation must consist of the biblical text of the *Arami oved
avi* passage. In a word, we engage in *mikra*. In this respect
the *hava'at bikkurim* and the Seder night are identical.

2) At this stage, however, the two rituals part company. In
the act of *hava'at bikkurim*, the Torah only required that a
text be recited. There is no requirement that it be translated
or elaborated upon. In contrast, on the Seder night there
are additional demands. The mitzva of *sippur y'tziat Mitzrayim*
at the Seder is basically an act of *talmud Torah*. *Talmud
Torah* involves within it elaboration and exegesis. The mishna
in *Pesaḥim* (10:4) mandates: "And he explains and elaborates
from *Arami oved avi* until he concludes the whole portion."
The Mishna speaks of "*limud*," which involves translation,
asking of questions and conceptualization. In fact, the core
of *Maggid* is a systematic exegesis and discussion of every
word of the *Arami oved avi* passage. We engage in a *Torah
she-b'al Peh* analysis of a *Torah she-biKHtav* text.

This analysis utilizes all the elements that comprise *Torah
she-b'al Peh*. For our purposes these elements may be
subdivided into Ihree different areas. The first is Midrash.
This refers to the exegesis of biblical verses in accordance
with the hermeneutical rules set down by our sages (e.g.,
the Thirteen *Middot* of Rabbi Yishmael, the Thirty-Two *Middot*
of Rabbi Eliezer).

The second category is Mishna. This refers to the set laws
and statements cited in the *mishnayot* and *memrot*.[11]

Finally, we have *gemara*, which refers to halakhic analysis
and conceptualization. Rashi in various places in the Talmud
translates *gemara* as the *s'varot*[12]—the logical basis for the
laws of the Mishna. However, the most full and eloquent
definition is given by Rambam in *Hilkhot Talmud Torah*
(1:11): "And one is obligated to apportion his time of study,
so that he spends one-third of his time studying *Torah
she-biKHtav*, another third studying *Torah she-b'al Peh*, and

one-third in understanding and trying to see the development from one step to another from beginning to end, and he should compare cases and derive one idea from another; these elements are called *gemara*."[13]

In the Haggada we find that all three areas of the oral law are used and applied. Firstly, we have Midrash. As was quoted above, the *Arami oved avi* passage is interpreted and explained through the different devices of Midrash. Secondly, the Haggada includes a number of passages of Mishna, of set halakhot and statements. Examples include the passage taken from the Mishna in *Pesaḥim* (10:5) "Rabban Gamliel used to say, anyone who has not said these three things at Passover has not fulfilled his obligation, etc.,"[14] and the response to he wise son "And you shall even tell him, (all the halakhot including) "We do not eat any food after the eating of the Afikoman,"[15] which is a law found in the Mishna in *Pesaḥim* (10:8). Finally, the Haggada contains elements of "*gemara*," of logical deductions and inferences. An example of this is the passage "Therefore, it is our duty to thank, praise . . ."[16] which is a logical conclusion based upon the reading of the immediately preceding halakhot (i.e., *Pesaḥ*, *Matzah* and *Maror*). Thus the Haggada not only involves *mikra*, but also *limud*. In fact the word Haggada and its root "*haged*" imply not only telling, but also an act of study and *talmud Torah*, as we find prior to *Matan Torah* when the Almighty commands Moshe, "Thus shall you say to the House of Yaakov and tell (*v'taggid*) to the Children of Israel" (Exodus 19:3)[17]

3) It is not enough, however, for the Jew to be a student the night of the Seder: he must also become a teacher. This reflects the third aspect of the Haggada—*masora*. The Jew must teach his children and others about the glorious event that occurred in Egypt long ago. The Haggada, before the passage about the four sons, included the portion "Blessed

be the Omnipotent. Blessed be He who hath given the Torah to his people Israel. Blessed be He, etc."[18] What, in fact, is this passage? In a word, it is a short version of *Birkat ha-Torah*[19]—the blessing made on the Torah. If we carefully examine the Torah blessings, in general, we see that they, too, stress the aspect of *masora*, the passing on of tradition. We state "And the house of Israel. And we and our children and our children's children should all be privileged to know your name, and be students of your Torah for its own sake."[20] Moreover, at the close of the blessing we say, "Blessed be the Lord, who teaches Torah to His people, Israel."[21] It is as if the Almighty himself becomes part of that *masora* community. After this blessing, the passage about the four sons, which concretizes the notion of teaching and passing on the story of the Exodus to one's children, each at his respective level, appears.

4) The fourth aspect is the "question and answer" style dialogue that is found in parts of the Haggada. Why is it so crucial that the child ask questions; why do we prompt him? Simply put, Judaism insists that God reveals himself to the man who seeks after and thirsts for God. The verse in Deuteronomy (4:29) reads: "But if you search there for the Lord your God, you will find him if only you will seek him with all your heart and soul."[22] We want to initiate the child into the *masora* community that seeks out the Almighty and yearns for his presence and illumination. We want the child to become a "*m'vakesh Hashem*"—"a seeker of God."

5) The fifth aspect of *sippur y'tziat Mitzrayim* is the central role that the meal and food play at the Seder. The drama of *sippur y'tziat Mitzrayim* begins with Kiddush and closes with *Nishmat* and *Yishtabah* after the meal. In fact, this is the reason that the *Shulhan Arukh* is so careful in specifying that the Kiddush on the night of the fifteenth of Nisan should be recited after astronomical nightfall.[23] (On other

festivals, one may usher in the festival and recite Kiddush earlier when it is still daytime.[24]) Kiddush is part of *sippur y'tziat Mitzrayim*, and therefore, must take place on the night of the fifteenth proper. Kiddush the night of *Pesaḥ* plays two roles. One is the normal role of Kiddush as the introduction of the festive meal as on every festival. Secondly, it is part of *sippur y'tziat Mitzrayim*. Kiddush contains within it the statement "who has chosen us from all nations,"[25] which is identical to the third language of *ge'ulat Mitzrayim* found in *Sidrat Va'era* (Exodus 6:6): "*V'lakaḥtī*"—"and shall take you unto me for a nation."

Moreover, there is another more basic reason for Kiddush playing a role in *sippur y'tziat Mitzrayim*. *Sippur y'tziat Mitzrayim* contains within it two elements. One is the recitation of certain passages. Second, is the element of performing certain actions, eating of certain foods, etc. When one eats matzah, *maror*, and *korban Pesaḥ* on the Seder night one fulfills these specific mitzvot. However, in addition. through the eating of these foods one is able to teach and convey the messages of *ge'ulat Mitzrayim*. They function as audio-visual aids in our educational scheme, namely, the Seder. This is what Rabban Gamliel was trying to convey[26] (in the Mishna [*Pesaḥim* 10:5] "Whoever has not said these three things has not fulfilled his obligation," etc.). He wanted the Jew, before he partakes of the foods, to explain their significance and message to all who are at this table. *Sippur y'tziat Mizrayim* is a careful blend, then, of narrative, teaching and actions to get across a unified message.

Kiddush also opens the *se'uda* every Shabbat and festival. Kiddush puts the meal in a context of holiness, uplifting it from a mundane effort to satisfy biological needs to the realm of the sacred. The idea of "a meal before God" is a fundamental one in Judaism.

It is along these lines that our sages spoke in saying "an

individual's table is an atonement for his sins" and "a dining table is similar to an altar."[27]

6) As was previously stated, the *mikra bikkurim* involves praise and thanksgiving to the Almighty. However, this is an awareness that comes about indirectly. The farmer recites the *Arami oved avi* passage which in itself, when understood, expresses gratitude. It is almost a notion of *"k'riyata zu hilula."*[28] The praise is implicit in the narration. In contrast, on the night of the Seder we are enjoined not only to praise and give gratitude, but also to break forth into spontaneous song—"Let us, therefore, sing a new song in his presence, Halleluyah."[29] The Jew's heart is overflowing with feelings of joy and thanksgiving. It is the night of the great romance between the Almighty and *K'nesset Yisrael*—"I am to my beloved and my beloved is to me."[30] It is these feelings that are expressed in the custom of reading the book of *Shir ha-Shirim* the night of the Seder. One can ask, philosophically, who is lowly man that he should have the audacity to praise God? Is not man "dust and ashes"? How then does he have the right to praise the infinite being, the Almighty? The halakha responds, True, philosophically there may be problems; however the Jew cannot contain himself. The Jew, on the night of the Seder, is overflowing with thanksgiving and song to God, and he cannot repress this authentic need to express his gratitude to the Holy one, Blessed be He.

7) As the Jew approaches the Story of the Exodus, there may be a tendency to look at the event as remote and distant from the here and now. Therefore, the Haggada contains within it three passages that help us deal with this problem. First of all, before the recitation of the *Arami oved avi* passage, we say: "And if God had not taken our ancestors out of Egypt, we and our children and our children's children would still be enslaved in Egypt."[31] We make a declaration of relevance. Why, in fact, are we discussing these events of

history; what is their relevance to our present situation? And to this we respond that were it not for the redemption in Egypt, there would be no Jewish People today.

Secondly, before Hallel we recite that "in every generation a person should look upon himself as if he personally had come out of Egypt. Not our ancestors alone did the Holy One, blessed be He, redeem, but us also He redeemed with them."[2] The events of *y'tziat Mitzrayim* are not only relevant to us; rather, we are actually reexperiencing history on the night of the Seder. It is a current as well as a historical event. This recognition enables us to recite *Hallel* and break forth into spontaneous song, because it is we who left Egypt as well.

Finally, we recite the "*v'hi she-amda*" passage: "For not only one tyrant has risen up against us to destroy us, but in every generation tyrants have sought to destroy us and the Holy One, Blessed be He, delivered us from their hands."[33] Not only do we relive the experience of Egypt, but we also realize that danger and annihilation threaten the Jewish people in every generation and locale. We move from the historical events to a better understanding of our current situation. The custom is that at this point in the Seder one lifts up his cup of wine. Why is this done? The cup is the symbol of Jewish destiny and eternity—*netzaḥ Yisrael*, as the verse " A cup of salvation I shall uplift, and call on the Almighty's name"[34] indicates. At the Seder we speak of the relevance of historical events, the reliving of those events and the cycle of danger and redemption that is characteristic of Jewish history.

8) The Mishna in *Pesaḥim* (10:5) dictates "and he explains the *Arami oved avi* passage until he completes it." However, in our Haggada we do not complete the passage in its totality. We do not recite and discuss the last verse and a half, which read: "He hath brought us into this place, and

hath given us this land, a land flowing (with) milk and honey. And now, behold, I have brought the first of the fruits of the land which Thou hast given to me, O Lord . . ." (Deuteronomy 26:9-10).35 The farmer bringing the *bikkurim* would include these verses and then set down the fruits "before the Lord your God."[36] It is understandable why the Haggada did not include the last verse that discusses the actual bringing of fruits, as that is out of place on the Seder night. However, why was the verse discussing the entry into the Land of Israel not included in our version of the Haggada? A number of approaches exist to resolve this problem. First of all, if we included this reference to the Land of Israel, we would convey the impression that there are five expressions of or references to *ge'ula* and not four (as we maintain). We would include "*v'heveti*" as one of the references to *ge'ula*, and *Hazal* felt that this would not be appropriate on the Seder night. Why is this the case? Firstly, the four references to *ge'ula* that were stated by the Almighty to Moshe in *Sidrat Vaera* were new ideas that had not been expressed to the Patriarchs. However, "*v'heveti*," "and I shall bring you into the land . . ." was already promised to Avraham, Yizhak, and Ya'akov individually in the *B'rit Avot*. They were already promised that their descendants would inherit the Land of Israel. Secondly, although the Jewish people did enter into the Land of Israel subsequent to the Exodus from Egypt, this was not the primary goal of *y'tziat Mitzrayim*. It was their destination but not their destiny. The direct goal of *y'tziat Mitzrayim* was the revelation at Sinai. The goal was the transformation of a subjugated people into "a nation of priests and a holy nation."[37] It was not just to grant them political and economic freedom, but also to create a sacred people. Moshe, at the episode of the burning bush, asked the Almighty: "Who (am) I that I should go unto Pharaoh, and that I should bring forth the Children of Israel out of

Egypt?" (Exodus 3:11).[38] And the Almighty gives an answer
that seems at first to be a bit difficult: "Certainly I will be
with you and this shall be unto you the sign that I have sent
you: When thou has brought forth the people out of Egypt
they shall serve God upon this mountain."[39] What was the
Almighty saying to Moshe; how did this answer his query?
The Almighty was stating, Know, Moshe, that the purpose
of ge'ulat Mitzrayim is not political and social freedom. For
that task, I would not have picked you. I did not pick you
to be a diplomat or a king or political leader. Rather, the
purpose of the Exodus is to create a holy nation, to make
them a Torah nation. For this purpose, God says, I need a
Rebbe, a teacher and mentor who will lead and guide this
people. And for this role, you are the best candidate. Pesaḥ
is the holiday of y'tziat Mitzrayim and leads into Shavuot
and matan Torah. These two festivals do not focus on the
Land of Israel as a central theme. According to Rambam in
Moreh Nevukhim, it is instead Sukkot that celebrates the
Land of Israel.[40]

Thirdly, it is possible to suggest that during the time the
Temple still stood, the text of the Haggada did include the
last verses relating to the entry into the Land of Israel. Upon
the destruction of the Temple and the subsequent exile,
Ḥazal changed the text in order to conform to the new
reality in which Am Yisrael found itself.

9) Finally, on the night of the Seder, the Jew mentions all
the wonderful things that the Almighty has done and is
doing for him and his people. This, in fact, is the thrust of
Birkat ha-Mazon and, therefore, it also functions as part of
sippur y'tziat Mitzrayim (in addition to its role as grace after
the meal.) After discussing God's special relationship with
the Jewish People we move to the Hallel ha-Gadol, which
contains a recognition of God's benevolence to the whole
world. We recognize and express gratitude for this, as we

state, "Who giveth food unto all flesh, for His kindness endures forever."[41] This leads us to the climax of the Seder. "*Nishmat*," when we speak of the future, the *Aharit ha-Yamim*, when all living beings shall give praise to the Almighty—"*Nishmat kol hai t'varekh* . . ."[42] These portions add a glorious eschatological dimension to the *shevah* and *hoda'a* sections that are so essential to the Haggada.

NOTES

1. "וענית ואמרת לפני ה' אלוהיך ארמי אבד אבי וירד מצרימה ויגר שם במתי מעט ויהי שם לגוי גדול עצום ורב. וירעו אותנו המצרים ויעננו ויתנו עלינו עבודה קשה. ונצעק אל ה' אלהי אבותינו וישמע ה' את קלנו וירא את ענינו ואת עמלנו ואת לחצנו. ויוצאנו ה' ממצרים ביד חזקה ובזרע נטויה ובמרא גדול ובאתות ובמפתים . . . "

2. פסחים פרק י, משנה ה. - "ודורש מארמי אובד אבי עד שגומר כל הפרשה כולה".

3. "מצוות עשה של תורה לספר בנסים ונפלאות שנעשו לאבותינו במצרים בליל חמשה עשר בניסן, שנאמר, זכור את יום הזה אשר יצאתם ממצרים . . . והוא שידרוש מארמי אובד אבי עד שיגמור כל הפרשה, וכל המוסיף ומאריך בדרוש פרשה זו, הרי זה משובח" (רמב"ם, הלכות חמץ ומצה, פרק, הלכה א, ד).

4. ופעמים אחדות הסביר רבנו שליט"א בכיוון אחר, שחז"ל ביססו את ההגדה על קטע זה של "מקרא ביכורים" מכיון שהינו נאמר בגוף ראשון, ולא בגוף שלישי כסיפור דברים. האדם מדבר כעד וכמאורע בענייניס, ובליל הסדר ההלכה דורשת ש"חייב אדם לראות את עצמו כאילו הוא יצא ממצרים". ולכן חז"ל בחרו בקטע זה, המדבר בגוף ראשון, כאלו כל השיעבוד וגאולה עבר עליו ממש.

5. "והגדת לבנך ביום ההוא לאמר, בעבור זה עשה ה' לי בצאתי ממצרים" (שמות יג, ח).

6. "שצוונו לספר ביציאת מצרים בליל ט"ו בניסן בתחילת הלילה כפי צחות לשון המספר . . . ולהודות לו, יתעלה על כל טוב שגמלנו" (ספר המצוות, מצווה קנז).

7. "לפיכך אנחנו חייבים להודות להלל לשבח לפאר לרומם להדר לברך לעלה ולקלס למי שעשה לאבותינו ולנו את כל הנסים האלה".

8. "שצוונו לספר טובותיו אשר היטיב לנו והצילנו . . . ולשבחו על כל זה ולבקש ממנו ולהתמיד הברכה כשיביא הביכורים" (ספר המצוות, קלב).

8. "הגדתי היום לה' אלוהיך" (דברים כו, ג).

10. "אודין ושבחינן יומא הדין קדם ד' אלקא . . . " וכן עיין באבן עזרא על אתר.

11. עיין בבא מציעא ל"ג ע"ב, וברש"י ד"ה הדר דרש להו הוי רץ למשנה.

12. עיין ברכות ה' ע"א, וברש"י ד"ה זה גמרא - "סברת טעמי המשנה שממנה יוצאה הוראה", ועיין עוד בבא מציעא ל"ג ע"א ד"ה גמרא "שהוא נותן לב להבין סתימות טעמי המשנה מה הם וכששתים סותרות זו את זו יבין לתרץ . . . "

13. "וחייב לשלם את זמן למידתו. שליש בתורה שבכתב, שליש בתורה שבעל פה, ושליש יבין וישכיל אחרית דבר מראשיתו ויוציא דבר מדבר וידמה דבר לדבר ויבין במדות שהתורה נדרשת בהן שידע היאך הוא עיקר המדות והיאך יוציא האסור והמותר וכיוצא בהן מדברים שלמד מפי השמועה. ועניין זה הוא הנקרא גמרא.

14. "רבן גמליאל היה אומר: כל מי שלא אמר שלשה דברים אלו בפסח לא יצא ידי חובתו ואלו הן פסח, מצה ומרור . . . "

15. "אין מפטירין אחר הפסח אפיקומן.

16. "לפיכך אנחנו חייבים להודות להלל . . . "

17. "כה תאמר לבית יעקב ותגיד לבני ישראל".

18. "ברוך המקום ברוך הוא, ברוך שנתן תורה לעמו ישראל, ברוך הוא".

19. עיין ב"הגדה שלימה" לרב מנחם מנדל כשר ז"ל, עמוד יח, הערה עט, המביא מדברי "שבולי הלקט", וזה לשונו: "לפי שרוצה לדרוש מקראות הללו הכתובים כנגד ארבעה בנים מתחיל בברכת התורה". ועיי"ש.

20. "והערב נא ה' אלוהינו את דברי תורתך בפינו ובפי עמך בית ישראל. ונהיה אנחנו וצאצאינו וצאצאי צאצאינו כולנו יודעי שמך ולומדי תורתך לשמה."

21. "ברוך אתה ה' המלמד תורה לעמו ישראל".

22. "ובקשתם משם את ה' אלוהיך ומצאת כי תדרשנו בכל לבבך ובכל נפשך". ועיין בספורנו על אתר - "והטעם שתמצאנו הוא כי אמנם תדרשנו בכל לבבך מרוב הצרות". וכן עיין שמות יח, טו "ויאמר משה לחותנו כי יבא אלי העם לדרוש אלוהים" וברמב"ן שם ד"ה "כי יבא".

23. "יהיה שולחנו ערוך כדי שיאכל מיד כשתחשך . . . אבל לא יאמר קידוש עד שתחשך" (שו"ע או"ח סימן תעב סעיף א). ועיין במ"ב שם.

24. ועיין בספר "המועדים בהלכה" לרב ש. י. זוין ז"ל, עמוד רסד.

25. "אשר בחר בנו מכל עם".

26. עיין בלשון הרמב"ם, פרק ז מהלכות חמץ ומצה הלכה א-ה, ש"יכל מי שלא אמר שלשה דברים אלו בט"ו לא יצא ידי חובתו ואלו הן פסח, מצה ומרור . . . ודברים אלו (כל מה שנכתב בהלכה א-ה) כולן נקראין הגדה". ועיין בגר"ח על השי"ט עמוד לג פיסקא "והגדת לבנך". (אולם עיין בדברי הרמב"ן במלחמות-ברכות, דף ב' ע"ב בדפי הרי"ף דמשמע דדינו של ר"ג נאמר במצוות הפרטיות ולא בדין סיפור יציאת מצרים).

27. ״שולחנו של אדם מכפר״ (ברכות נה).

28. קריאתא זו הילולא (מגילה י״ד ע״א).

29. ״ונאמר לפניו שירה חדשה הללויה״.

30. ״אני לדודי ודודי לי״ (שיר השירים ו, ג).

31. ״ואלו לא הוציא הקב״ה את אבותינו ממצרים הרי אנו ובנינו ובני בנינו משועבדים היינו לפרעה במצרים״.

32. ״בכל דור ודור חייב אדם לראות את עצמו כאלו הוא יצא ממצרים שנאמר: והגדת לבנך ביום ההוא לאמר בעבור זה עשה ה׳ לי בצאתי ממצרים. לא את אבותינו בלבד גאל הקב״ה, אלא אף אותנו גאל עמהם . . . ״

33. ״והיא שעמדה לאבותינו ולנו שלא אחד בלבד עמד עלינו לכלותינו אלא שבכל דור ודור עומדים עלינו לכלותינו, והקב״ה מצילנו מידם״.

34. ״כוס ישועות אשא ובשם ה׳ אקרא״ (תהלים קטז, יג).

35. ״ויביאנו אל המקום הזה ויתן לנו את הארץ הזאת ארץ זבת חלב ודבש. ועתה הנה הבאתי את פרי האדמה אשר נתתה לי ה׳ . . . ״

36. ״והנחתו לפני ה׳ אלוהיך והשתחוית לפני ה׳ אלוהיך״ (שם).

37. ״ממלכת כהנים וגוי קדוש״ (שמות יט, ו).

38. ״ויאמר משה אל האלהים מי אנכי כי אלך אל פרעה וכי אוציא את בני ישראל ממצרים״.

39. ״ויאמר כי אהיה עמך, וזה לך האות כי אנכי שלחתיך בהוציאך את העם ממצרים תעבדון את האלהים על ההר הזה״.

40. ״ואשר נראה לי בארבעה מינין שבלולב, שהיא שמחה וששון על יציאתם מן המדבר שלא היה מקום זרע ותאנה וגפן ורמון ומים אין לשתות, אל מקום עצי פרי ונהרות, לפיכך נלקח לזיכרון לכך הנאה שבכיותיה, ובעל הריח טוב, והעלים הנאים וגם הנאה שבעשבותיה, כלומר ערבי נחל . . . ״ (רמב״ם, מורה נבוכים, חלק ג, פרק מג, מהדורת רב קאפח).

41. ״נותן לחם לכל בשר כי לעולם חסדו״.

42. נשמת כל חי תברך את שמך אלוהינו . . . ״

A Eulogy for
R. Hayyim Heller

This essay contains an analysis of *avelut* and our relationship to the dead; a statement of the significance of communion between generations; and a moving evaluation of R. Hayyim Heller, his personality and his way of thinking Several footnotes of halakhic interest can be found in the original Hebrew version, published in *Divrei Hagut veHa'arkha*. The translation is dedicated to the memory of David Carmy *z"l*.

I. "The Reward of the Eulogy—the Mournful Cry"

Although the eulogy (*hesped*) is one aspect of *avelut*, it differs in its legal manifestations from *avelut*, which is expressed through *shiva* and *sh'loshim*.

1. The obligation of *shiva* and *sh'loshim* devolves only upon the immediate family while the obligation of the eulogy includes the distant as well. Our Sages spoke severely of neglect in eulogizing a scholar or, for that matter, any decent person.

2. The act of eulogizing, as opposed to the *avelut* of *sh'loshim* and *shiva*, is not is not defined by specific acts. The external act of eulogizing, of enunciating words of grief and lamentation, is no more than an instrument through which the goal is realized—"grief or heartfelt sorrow."

The phrase "grief or heartfelt sorrow" (*avelut o aninut shebalev*) indicates a dual act—intellectual and emotional. "Heart," as a figure of speech, is the subject of objective cognition and subjective experience. Mourning in the heart evolves, in rectilinear fashion, from the cognition to the experience. Its point of origin is the honest inspection of

46

the character of the deceased, with its specific nature and all its abilities, its powers, and its virtues, from which arises the valuation of his importance as individual and as social man in his life, and the greatness of loss in his absence. The telos of mourning is the total spiritual shudder of the mourners, the eruption of the experience of suffering, which is replaced by a grasp of the vacuity and desolation of human existence in general and the whole tragedy connected with the loss of a human being and the absence of a friend in particular.

It is therefore the duty of the eulogist to describe completely and concisely, in logical, incisive categories, the full stature of the deceased, to stress the whole wonder woven into that concrete, personal reality, with which we have shared, so to speak, "a lodging for the night," and also to project, with the dimensions of an alert sensitivity, the sorrow arising, in all its realness and direness, from that opaque event we call death. The eulogist is an excellent pedagogue, the agent of a cool, calm intellect, but he is also an artist, representing the frenzied experience of the man who stands before something opaque and dreadful. The eulogist explains and interprets, portrays and creates. Clear understanding is transmuted with emotional impression—"the reward of the eulogy is the mournful cry" (*B'rakhot* 6b). The tremor of the soul, as revealed in the cry, the voice uplifted in mourning, is the root, the innermost part of the eulogy. "Be fervent in my eulogy, as I will be there" (*Shabbat* 153a). Speak the words of eulogy with an honest true recognition, but also with heart-warming feelings: my image will stand before you: do not distort it by exaggeration or understatement, indifference or cheap sentimentality.

Therefore, determined the Rabbis as halakha and as *mussar,* that "Just as the dead are punished, so are the eulogists and those who respond to them" (*B'rakhot* 62a). The eulogy, intellectually speaking, must excel in exactitude and objectivity. One may not overstate the truth or minimize it. Excess or deficiency both lead to deformation of the likeness.

II. "From Afar the Lord Appeared to Me"

Grief within the heart is rooted in man's queer nature as an axiological creature and in his particular retrospective act: "From afar the Lord appeared to me; and with an everlasting love I have loved thee" (Jeremiah 31:2). I see God far far away from me. At an immeasurable distance my eyes were opened. Once He was close, but then I was blind. I therefore forfeited His nearness; He became hidden from me. As long as the Creator was near, His *Shekhina* hovering over me, I did not sense the shining happiness streaming from this wondrous closeness. When I kept Shabbat and *moadim*, when I wore tefillin, prayed, sanctified my life, my ways, my activities, I was often bereft of the sense of majesty with which my life was infused; I did not properly value all the sublimity and the clear light, flowing over a God-nourished reality. I did not always rejoice over the ability given me to stand before my Creator and to cleave unto Him. That I, a mortal, denizen of a house of clay, may enter the House of God, to subjugate myself to His infinite will, is the greatest *ḥesed* I have received. Spiritual boredom, however, ground this *ḥesed* under the wheels of a fast-moving and tasteless life, sin, and alienation from my Creator. I, the creature, squandered His nearness; I lost everything. I remained utterly alone, exiled, and banished, in sempiternal ruin. I have nobody to plead with, nobody to cry to from the depths. The gates of heaven are closed to me; my path is twisted. But suddenly the wonder takes place; my consciousness is shaken to the foundations. "From afar the Lord appeared to me." From an infinite distance breaks forth the image of the *Shekhina* I had exiled from my home, I hear the soft whisper of consoling tidings from an awe-suffused silence: "An everlasting love I have loved thee!" I, the homesick sinner, begin to sense the ugliness of a pitiful, impoverished, God-separated existence, as against the heartening brightness of an existence filled with the glory of His majesty. I see from afar, and the distance intensifies my longing . . . The separation was easy; the rapprochement is difficult. My going away was simple; the turning on my heel is difficult and severe. Nevertheless, my eyes are to God and His *Shekhina*; I will not cease seeking; otherwise my life is frenzied and tempest-tossed. The distance enchants, captures my heart, dragging me onward, onward . . .

The same tragic paradox is true of our relation to a great man. So long as he is in our midst, we meet him in the street and salute him, we hear what he says and gaze upon his face, we are not aware of the great *ḥesed* which God granted us, enabling us to be with him. With gelid heart, stupidly, we fail to notice him, passing on to our gray routine and trivial habits. Suddenly the man departs to other worlds and a different realm of being, and his image begins to attract us from mystery-draped distances like a nitid star twinkling from a sky of midnight blue. Suddenly we fix a longing gaze on the beautiful, captivating image. We stretch out our arms to embrace it, but an infinite gap stretches between us. Just a moment ago he was so close. Then we didn't notice, only now we begin to yearn. But it is too late for longing. We are swept powerfully toward someone who is no longer to be found. The eulogy is the recognition of the person and the desire for him after he has slipped away; it is the absurd will to turn the third person into the second person, having betrayed the real live presence when it faced us. Mourners and eulogists occupy themselves with the building of bridges across that gap that will never be bridged. Nevertheless, it is this "absurd" that is the essence of mourning in the heart. The disciples of Elijah went out to seek their master after his ascension in the tempest. Three days they sought him upon mountains and in valleys. They sought him but they did not find him.

III. "It Happened at the Inn"

How beautiful the midrash (*Bereshit Rabba* on *Miketz*) "When R. Simon died, R Levi said: Joseph's brethren found something, yet Scripture states: 'Their heart went out'; we, who have sustained the loss of R Simon, how much more!"

Finding the money in their sacks caused the brothers great fear. A deathly dread leapt upon them. A small error of timing brought them to this anguish. Had they opened their bags immediately after they left Egypt, they would never have been tortured by the fear of false accusation. They could have returned the money to that queer person, to straighten things out. But they tarried a bit in checking their sacks, and when they did, they were already far away. "It happened on the way, at the inn, that one opened his bag . . . and saw his money." It would be a long way back. To return would be difficult; to approach the strange viceroy, dangerous. The direct way to rectify the mistake was blocked. Therefore, their hearts went out and they trembled. The Rabbis evaluated the reaction of the brothers to the finding of the money: "They should have checked their sacks before leaving—had they been given wheat or barley !"

A shaft of bitter irony is apparent in R. Levi's eulogy for R. Simon. Here we are, "at the inn," says the eulogist. R Simon has disappeared: a living bond is snapped, the friendship is over. There were better days; then the distant R. Simon was very near. But then we didn't bother to understand him properly. We hadn't the leisure to study his face. Only now, when we have lost him, do we try to find him; we sit and wonder: This R. Simon—who was he? Who was this wondrous individual? Now we open the sack—the casket—of R. Simon and stare at it, trembling. Now we discover the treasure, hidden from us all that time that he dwelt among us. But this recognition came too late. Again the tragic paradox of the prophet of destruction: "From afar the Lord appeared to me; and with everlasting love I have loved thee." We raised our eyes to unlimited spaces, beyond our conception, to confront one who has thither withdrawn.

IV. "The Remnant of Their Scribes"

Who was this man who departed us in silence and graceful humility? Who was R. Hayyim (Heller), who did not accept a public position and who had no use for the customary titles, his entire greatness being expressed in two simple words: "Reb Hayyim"?

Several years ago, at one of the *Haggei Semikha* of RIETS, when Rabbi Samuel Belkin introduced R. Hayyim to the large congregation in the packed hall, he quoted from *Sh'mone Esre*: "the righteous . . . and the elders of thy people the House of Israel and the remnant of their scribes"; "R. Hayyim," continued Rabbi Belkin, "is one of the remnant of the scribes of Israel." In this he truly captured what was unique about the man! I was sitting on the dais, next to R. Hayyim, and I noticed him, introverted, closed in himself, singed as it were by the glances of the people; on his face, the sad perplexity of a lonely man pushed willy-nilly into the midst of a noisy, boisterous crowd. I asked myself: Why did the redactors of the prayers use this phrase? Why not simply: "for their scribes?" According to tradition, the *Sh'mone Esre* was formulated twice: at the time of Ezra and at Yavneh. During both periods the Jewish community was full of scribes and sages. Why did the formula of the *b'rakha* emphasize the remnant of past generation, instead of praying for the welfare of present sages and scribes?

The answer is not, I believe, esoteric. It does not matter

how many *talmidei hakhamim, g'dolim,* or writers, with all
the sweep and scope of their Torah creativity, a generation
is blessed with—it cannot be linked to the great chain of
Tradition unless it includes a remnant of scribes from the
lofty past, bridging the gap between generations. There can
only be Tradition where the individual becomes the interaction
of eras. To transmit and to receive is to enfold the generations
in the religious present; "now" is to be anchored in "once."
In every generation we meet, miraculously, the soul of an
ancient generation planted in the present, emanating the
aura of the venerable, the beauty of age. Living figures
wander; they roam from generation to generation. Tradition
includes not only theoretical innovations, abstract concepts,
halakhic formulas, and logical principles, but also types of
being, feelings, and reactions: a certain existential rhythm
and experiential continuity. One cannot achieve a full tradition
without personal *d'vekut* to a previous generation. In each
and every era, we, the receivers, need at least one individual
who can connect the generations, one individual about whom
we can say, Here is the witness to the lofty events of the
distant past; "Your eyes seeing your teachers," so to say.

   This is the primary motif of the legend that Serach, daughter
of Asher, survived until the times of Moses (*Sota* 13a; according
to another legend, she lived even longer). Even the generation
of Moses, the miraculous generation of the Exodus, that
witnessed Sinai and accepted the Torah, needed an ancient
figure, Serach daughter of Asher, who in childhood sat in
grandfather's lap and amused herself with the hair of his
head and his beard. Without her, the personal continuity of
generations would have been broken. Moses himself
proclaimed in his song: "This is my God. . .the God of my
fathers, and I shall exalt Him." Even if we are greatly loved
by Him, even if He revealed Himself to us on the sea and in
Egypt, we must still confront the image of our forefathers

and introduce them into our consciousness. One cannot say "This is my God" unless the song of the present is entwined with that of the past: the God of my fathers. Only an aged mother, her back bent and her cheeks furrowed, who once called an old man "Grandfather," knows the mystery of linked generations, the binding of those times with these.

And if this was so at the time of Moses, how much more so in our generation, which has witnessed the erosion of the pillars of tradition. When the few must struggle against the many, the need to draw yeoman's courage from the living tradition as it is reified in a real personality attired in the majesty of time—a mediation, a bridge between fathers and sons, between strength and weakness—becomes much greater. Under such conditions, the trembling, wrinkled handshake with its rhythm of generations; the fatherly or motherly glance in which abides the mystery of the past; the strains of a tremulous voice, in which is preserved the silence of Eternity; tales of strange and wondrous persons, of events wrapped in the mist of passing time—these can turn the balance in favor of *kodesh* against *ḥol*. Not for nothing did the Rambam stress (Introduction to the *Yad*, citing *Baba Batra* 122b) that "Ahiya ha-Shiloni . . . was a Levite, and studied under Moses, and was a child in the time of Moses." This statement is very important. A generation that saw the breakdown of *Bet David*, the erection of two golden calves, needed Ahiya ha-Shiloni, who had raced, leapt, played in Moses' courtyard (he was a Levite and lived in the camp of Levites), who had run after him in the spacious desert, who strode with him, hand in hand, on yellow, sunburnt sand. Only such a man, a prophet of God, a vestige of an ancient era, a remnant of the scribes of the past, could fortify weak knees and revive the hearts of the despondent.

Rabbi Belkin was right to call Rav Hayyim one of the remnant of scribes. A spark from the soul of Ahiya ha-Shiloni, who had clung to Moses as a child, sank into his soul. As long as R. Hayyim was with us, among us, there existed a strong tie between us and earlier generations. When he went away, the knot was undone . . . He [R. Hayyim] had perpetual discussions with them [g'dolim with whom R. Hayyim was close]. When I visited him at home, on the West Side of Manhattan, with its congeries of bustling, hollow, Jewish life; with its synagogues, societies, clubs, and their auxiliaries, I always felt as if I were entering another world, as if I had breached some border separating two realms of being—the domain of earlier generations, of Shakh, Taz, and Gra, and that of modern Orthodoxy, with its snipped wings and rootlessness, unable to fathom the depths of religious experience. When I opened the door to his room, I found him in his old armchair, spectacles on his nose, engrossed in *Bet ha-Levi, Meshiv Davar,* or *Malbushei Yomtov.* When he noticed me, he did not cease his thinking. With a slight smile and the motion of a finger, he invited me to sit down next to him. Sometimes I didn't know if he was aware of my presence or not. He was totally involved in his dialogue with one of that *havura,* in which, as a child, he had found himself. His facial expressions, with their mixture of good humor and melancholy, indicated something of the content of that conversation. Sometimes he nodded his head, his face exuding satisfaction, as if in agreement with the absent friend; sometimes he raised his eyebrows with wonder, stretched the fingers of his right hand as if to ask: Is it possible that R. Shabtai (Shakh) differs?! When R. Hayyim told stories about *g'dolei Yisrael,* whether he had known them or they had been dead for centuries, he uttered, not desiccated words, but living experiences full of warmth and movement . . . Moved by old, forgotten tales, he chuckled and sorrowed with his heroes. Images he described came to life, pushed their way into his modest room. Do you know

where this power came from? Not from any art of speech or
of imagery! He never used a metaphor. He lived the events
he recounted. He himself belonged to those generations,
whose greatness he transmitted to us. He spoke their language
and understood their spirit. A lonely wanderer in the lanes
of the present, at home in the near and distant past—that
was who he was. There was something special about him,
something that flowed from the days when there were spiritual
giants in the land, the men of name in the world of Torah.
O he was a remnant of the ancient scribes

V. "Why Were the Ancients Called Scribes?"

What is the meaning of the word *sofrim* (scribes)? The
Talmud (*Kiddushin* 30a) gives this answer: "Why were the
ancients called *sofrim?*—Because they counted [*safru*] all the
letters in the Torah." Only one who is so knowledgeable
that he can count the letters, has the ability to join the rare
society of *sofrim.* R. Hayyim fulfilled this condition. He
knew so much! He could be precise not only with the text
of a *tosafot* but also with a phrase in *Me'irat Enayim* or
Shakh. His two-volume *Le-Hikre Halakhot* on *Hoshen Mishpat,*
attests to his unusual knowledge. He was faithful in the
entire mansion of halakha, including the later works of
Sephardic *g'dolim* (many of whom are quoted in *Shakh* on
Hoshen Mishpat), whose very names escape us. Many times
he pointed out to me the nuances of these books, a slight
emendation of style that resolved the difficulties of criticism.

However, there is another definition of *sofrim. Yer. Shekalim*
explains, "Because they enumerated the whole Torah (*mis-
parim*)." On this view it is not enough to know the letters.
The crown of *sofrim* only befits one for whom halakhot are
organized and fluent. Understanding of learning, classification,
organization—not only external knowledge—present the
scholar with the honorable title of *sofer.* R. Hayyim knew

how to enumerate his Torah. He was an expert at classification and systematic method. He always began by clarifying the text and distillation of verbal forms: then he turned to conceptual analysis. He began by counting letters—and ended with systematic enumeration.

VI. "The Long Formula and the Short Formula"

In halakhic research, as in *b'rakhot*, there are two forms: the long formula and the short formula. These symbolize, so to say, two forms of *kappara* in the *Mikdash* (See *Yoma* 58b). According to R. Eliezer: the *kohen*, when sprinkling the blood of the "inner" sin offerings on the gold altar in the *heikhal*, would stand in one place. When blood of the "outer" sin offerings was sprinkled in the *azara*, the *kohen* would walk around the Altar, from corner to corner. *Avoda* on the inside (*heikhal*) is characterized by the short formula—the *kohen* does not walk around the *mizbe'ah*. On the outside (*azara*), we find the long formula—he must walk around the *mizbe'ah*; the former finished their work straightaway, the latter needed to walk around. There are analogously, two ways of studying Torah: There are those who, like the *kohanim* in the *azara*, exhaust the matter on foot, so to say; moving from corner to corner, from problem to problem, until halakhic truth is revealed. This is the long formula. The *kohanim* of the *heikhal* do not need this indirect path. They immediately touch the heart of the matter. Without moving from their place, without the complications of extraneous *pilpul*, within a short time stands the halakha, so unclear a moment ago, as if illuminated by a spotlight. Both formulae—the long and the short—are the words of living God; but from the pedagogic viewpoint, one prefers brevity to length, concentration to diffusions. R. Hayyim's formula was exceptionally short. He had a definite logical simplicity, which he used as a shortcut to reach an unperplexed, confident, halakhic conclusion.

VII. "Is there a Man Who Can Formulate the Benediction of the Heretics?"

A

This R. Hayyim was chosen by Providence and equipped to accomplish a difficult task. In order to grasp the nature of this task we must turn to our history and understand it within an historical context. The *baraita* (*B'rakhot* 28b) tells us: "Simon Pakuli prepared eighteen benedictions before Rabban Gamaliel. Said Rabban Gamaliel to the Rabbis: 'Is there a man who can formulate the benediction of heretics?' Sh'muel ha-Katan stood up and formulated it." One's impression is that the benediction of the heretics (*birkhat ha-minim*) aroused difficulties that had not existed previously, when the other eighteen were formulated. Rabban Gamaliel, we are told, needed to proclaim-request that someone step forward for the task, and that only one man was fit to undertake it. What does this mean?

At the time of Rabban Gamaliel in Yavneh there occurred a turning point in the struggle of loyal Jewry with the movement that would betray the tradition and the uniqueness of the nation. The dimensions of the struggle were fundamentally altered. Active conflict replaced passive shutting of eyes. The major reason for this was the terrible calamity that descended upon the nation with the destruction of the Temple. In truth, the flourishing of heretics in this generation was nothing new or startling. The contempt of enemies within was an old story in the annals of the Jewish people. Opponents of Judaism were particularly active during the Second Commonwealth. The Mishna (*Yoma* 18b) tells us that the high priest was sworn on Yom Kippur Eve that he would not conduct himself as a Sadducite: so great were the breaches in loyalty to the tradition, even among the sons of Aharon. Yet no benediction was formulated with reference to these scoffers and heretics. Why? Because the Rabbis were blessed with great patience. They were not among those eager for the destruction of sinners, however these may plot the distortion of our religious reality. Prayer is founded, according to halakha, on the attribute of mercy. (*B'rakhot* 20b and 26a). "Eighteen benedictions correspond to eighteen Tetragrammatons in Psalm 29" (*B'rakhot* 28b). Each benediction reflects the revealed-concealed light, shining from the letters of the Tetragrammaton, the nature of which is great mercy, delicate, pure love, grace, and peace. We plead with God for succor, health, and salvation; vindictiveness does not cry from our throats. Even when the Jew enumerates his cares, tells his Heavenly Father of his oppression and penury, his loneliness, the denial of his rights, his humiliation and insult, the malice of his enemies (in "*Re'e na be-onyenu*"), the cry for revenge is not heard. He prays for himself and his people but does not mention his malefactors, does not ask of God to do to them what they wished upon him and did to him. When and how will the evil be judged? The praying Jew had not thought about them; he ignored them, swallowed his agony and anger. Even when their image confronted him in full height, he did not raise his voice, bitterly, before God, but prayed that they return to their Jewish source, and to their Divine root, that they may cease their evil. Post-Maccabean Jewry preferred, under certain circumstances, to ignore evil, rather than to attack it frontally. Evil, idolatry, is called "*elilim*," lacking reality and value, concern with which is a waste of time, and of physical and spiritual forces, so to say "Do not answer a fool according to his folly."

Until the age of Rabban Gamaliel, the Sages of Israel, with their penetrating historical insight, tended to ignore evil, to hope that it would cease of itself. Then came the *ḥurban*, the nation was drenched in blood, Jerusalem was a pile of ruins, the spiritual centers were destroyed, and the best of her sons were dead. The enemy within betrayed Israel at this time of chaos. The antagonism against the tradition and the continuation of Jewish existence as a unique destiny reached new heights. Many apostates made peace with the foreign oppressor, spread malice against the people, plotted its spiritual and physical death. "*Elilim*" suddenly had become "alien gods," with power and rule. Our Sages felt, that in these circumstances it was impossible to shut one's eyes to the *minim*. With regard to *elilim* one could fulfill the scriptural verse "Thou shalt not turn to them"—that is, do not pay attention to them; but they could not be silent in the face of the satanic attack organized by "alien gods." The struggle was joined; the framework of prayer was broadened. Not only help, salvation, forgiveness, were subjects of prayer, but also the flattening of wicked pride. Judaism demanded active participation in its *polemos* against the treacherous movement. True, the idea of prayer stems from *ḥesed* and *raḥamim*; but these, too, are at war with evil! They sought and found a proof (in Psalm 29): "The God of majesty thundered over many waters." Even the attribute of *ḥesed* sometimes thunders over the waters of wickedness and struggles against them. A determination, with weighty consequences, was proclaimed by Rabban Gamaliel: *Rabbotai*, the time has come to formulate a benediction for heretics! Who is the man who has the power to formulate it?

B

For whom was Rabban Gamaliel searching? What did he expect of the man whose spirit would move him to innovate this benediction? One can answer this question, if one sees it against the backdrop of the metaphysical concept of the personality within Judaism. Man is created in the image of God. He carries within him the perpetual revelation of God to His creatures. The vectors of essence and character that are hidden in man, with all their variety, flow from a transcendent source. Therefore it is the obligation of the creature to become like the Creator, to imitate the ways of His Revelation: "As He is Graceful and Merciful, so you be graceful and merciful." The spiritual tendencies with which man was blessed express his participation in the infinite attributes of God. Judaism, through this ethical-metaphysical perspective, viewed its great representatives as bearers of His Majesty. One personality may shine with the attribute of *ḥesed*; another may demonstrate those of *g'vura* and absolute justice. Sometimes one meets a wonderful individual in which *ḥesed* and *din* have met, and formed one perfect whole. In Abraham was revealed pure *ḥesed*; in Isaac was bared *g'vura*; in Jacob, *tiferet*. Our Sages saw in Moses, the master of prophets, and his brother, the high priest, the realizations of *ḥesed* and truth, justice and peace. The candle of God is lit in the soul of each of the *g'dolei Yisrael*, and each wanders in his special path for his rendezvous with God.

C

The man whom Rabban Gamaliel invited to formulate the benediction of heretics was totally grasped by the attribute of *ḥesed*. It flowed from him forcefully and with boldness. If the force of circumstances necessitated a deviation from consistent mercifulness and affection to all flesh, to stand courageously and heroically against a hard, dastardly enemy, distorting the face of the nation and its faith—then the permission to lead the assault could only be given to a man, whose soul had sucked from the sources of *ḥesed* rather than *g'vura*. Only such a man could formulate the benediction of heretics to demand of his Heavenly Father the cessation of evil and destruction of the wicked. They found Sh'muel ha-Katan, whose motto was the verse "When thine enemy falters do not rejoice, and when he stumbles, do not let thy heart be merry" (*Avot* 4:9). Sh'muel, the ḥasid and the humble, who had never tasted the desire to settle accounts with malefactors, who had never complained about insults caused him, was chosen to fulfill this necessary task. This man, overflowing with *ḥesed*, forgiveness to all men, stood in the presence of the *Nasi* and coined a new benediction for the *Sh'mone Esre*. This benediction, which cries to God for the destruction of evil, grew from the soil of love and *ḥesed*. It was directed against evil and the reign of wickedness in their ideal form, so to say "May sin cease; not sinners."

D

What happened to fathers is a sign for the sons. We Jews, observant of Torah and mitzvot, have suffered a lot from the new heresy of biblical criticism, which aimed to dissolve the tradition, to breach the external covenant between nation and Torah. For many years we tried to ignore the evil, to eliminate it from our public arena. This method of indifference proved its utility over a long period, as long as the Jewish people vibrated with living religiosity and did not attend to blasphemous words. But times changed. What was permissible when traditional Jewry stood firm, *minut* blazing only at the periphery of the camp, cannot be done at a time when spiritual schism has reached its apex. We are again witnesses to the transformation of *elilim* into "alien gods." There was no choice: ignorance of evil must be replaced by destruction of evil.

Judaism found itself in the narrow pass; it was impossible to evade confrontation with the enemy at the gate: "Is there one who can formulate a benediction for heretics?"; is there one who can indicate the errors, the forgeries, the calculated conspiracy against our spiritual existence, that derive from this heretical literature? R. Hayyim *z"l* was the Sh'muel ha-Katan of our generation! Providence elected him for this task not merely for his intellectual qualifications, but for his great soul, entirely suffused with nobility and love and mercy for all creatures in the Divine Image. He was charitable in his person, in his pocket, even in his speech. His whole life-style was sensitivity and fatherly goodness. I never heard him use derogatory language. He never cursed another or called names. Others, at times, abused him, hurt him, but he did not complain or speak badly of them. When he recalled such an unpleasant episode, his eyes were dimmed by a heavy sadness, expressing pain and sorrow. He was trained in suffering, knowing how to suffer with a smile, to suffer and to laugh. Who like him fulfilled the words of the Mishna (*B'rakhot* 9:5): " 'With thy all'—with all measures that are measured thee." Sh'muel ha-Katan of our generation was appointed by Providence to coin the benediction of the heretics. Only he, who radiated freshness, joy, love, was qualified for this difficult work.

VIII. "Israel was a Lad; and I Loved Him"

Why was Sh'muel given the nickname "ha-Katan"? This epithet can be given four meanings: (1) shortness of physical stature; (2) humility, he made himself small (*Yerushalmi*, end of *Sota*); (3) relative stature—compared to the prophet Samuel (*Yer.* ibid.); (4) childlikeness ("*katan*" in the sense of a child). If we accept the fourth interpretation, we can exchange the phrase "Sh'muel ha-Katan" for a new phrase: Sh'muel the Child.

A strange polarity characterizes the world of authentic Judaism. It swings like a pendulum between the two ideals of maturity and childishness. The great man, whose intellect has been raised to a superior level through the study of Torah, gifted with well-developed, overflowing, powers—depth, scope, sharpness—should not be viewed as the totally adult. The soul of a child still nestles within him. On the one hand, he is knowledge-sated, strong of intellect, rich in experience, sober-sighted, crowned with age, great of spirit. On the other hand, he remains the young and playful child; naive curiosity, natural enthusiasm, eagerness and spiritual restlessness, have not abandoned him. If a man has aged and become completely adult, if the morning of life has passed him by and he stands, in spirit and soul, at his high noon, bleached of the dew of childhood, if he has grown up completely, in thinking, feeling, desire, trust—he cannot approach God. The adult is too clever. Utility is his guiding light. The experience of God is not a businesslike affair. Only the child can breach the boundaries that segregate the finite from the infinite. Only the child with his simple faith and fiery enthusiasm can make the miraculous leap into the bosom of God. "Israel was a lad and I loved him" (Hosea 11:1): "Is Ephraim my dear son, a playful child, that when I speak of him, I remember him again" (Jeremiah 31:19). The giants of Torah—when it came to faith, became little children, with all their ingenuousness, gracefulness, simplicity, their tremors of fear, the vivid sense of experience to which they are devoted. Where you find their maturity you find their childlike quality. What was my grandfather, R. Hayyim of Brisk? On the one hand, he was a great abstract thinker, who introduced basic conceptual transformations in the field of halakhic methodology. On the other hand, he was a child, unable to restrain his warm emotions, his yearning for something beautiful and elevated, his dreams and hopes. He, the man of iron discipline in the intellectual sphere, who captured the richness of halakha in acute, exact, logical molds, was swept without reservation in a bold stream of simplicity, innocence, sensitivity, perplexity, childish confusion, but also immeasurable confidence: R. Hayyim ha-Katan! What was my father *z"l*? A genius and a child! Supersensitive powers of abstraction and the innocence of a babe. A spark from the soul of the master of prophets, the father of sages in all generations, is contained in the soul of all *g'dolei Yisrael*. "She opened and showed the child; and behold, it was a crying lad." The whimper of a baby rent the air on the shore of the Nile. But it was not only then that Moses cried. Whenever he fell before God, he cried like a child. Who can fall before his father, raise his eyes to him alone, to seek consolation and salvation, if not the child! The weeping of a child accompanied *Rabbam shel Yisrael* from the Nile to Sinai, to the Tabernacle, to Nevo. Only the child could cry, could shed a tear. The mature, the adult, are not capable of the all-embracing, all-penetrating outpouring of soul. The most sublime crown we can give a great man, sparkles with the gems of childhood. It is not strange, therefore, that this crown was offered Sh'muel with the epithet "ha-Katan."

R. Hayyim Heller *z"l* also united the two poles: intellectual greatness and innocence of heart, unusual knowledge of Torah and the delightful simplicity of a small boy. Our own "Sh'muel ha-Katan" knew nothing of politics, infighting, formality, or ceremony. He never said anything to gain another's approval or to impress a crowd. His language was not decorative or flowery; he did not use fancy phrases to lend his ideas a meaningless luster. He detested complicated terminology. When I asked him to cut down on the quantity of material presented in his lectures in order to improve the format so that his listeners might be able to assimilate his rich bounty, he refused. "Give them, R. Hayyim, a little bit, let them digest your words," I said to him. "What do you want, R. Yoshe Ber, that I waste time, mislead people?" he would answer. He once told me that he had resigned the rabbinate of Lomz, because he felt that as a communal *rav*, things he disapproved of would be forced upon him and upon his leadership. "It states in Proverbs (3:4)," he ended this conversation, "'He shall find favor . . . in the eyes of God and man.'" Man must seek to fulfill his obligations before God, then he should find favor in the eyes of man. Inverting the order, one loses both worlds.

A Eulogy for
the Talner Rebbe

This reproduced lecture is a eulogy delivered by Rabbi Soloveitchik for Rabbi M. Z. Twersky *z"l*, the Talner Rebbe.

Aninut

There are two distinct phases in the process of mourning. The halakha has meticulously insisted upon their strict separation.

The first phase begins with death (of the relative for whom one is obliged to mourn) and ends with burial. With regard to Temple service, *aninut* continues through the day and following night. The second commences with burial and lasts seven or (with regard to some aspects) thirty days.

The first we call *aninut*; the second—*avelut*. What is the halakhic and experiential distinction between these two phases of mourning?

Aninut represent the spontaneous human reaction to death. It is an outcry, a shout, or a howl of grisly horror and disgust. Man responds to his defeat at the hands of death with total resignation and with an all-consuming masochistic, self-devastating black despair. Beaten by the fiend, his prayers rejected, enveloped by a hideous darkness, forsaken and lonely, man begins to question his own human singular reality. Doubt develops quickly into a cruel conviction and doubting man turns into mocking man.

At whom does man mock: At himself! He starts downgrading, denouncing himself. He dehumanizes himself. He arrives at the conclusion that man is not human, that he is just a living creature like the beast in the field. In a word, man's initial response to death is saturated with malice and ridicule toward himself. He tells himself: If death is the final destiny of all men, if everything human terminates in the narrow dark grave, then why be a man at all? Then, why make the pretense of being the choicest of all creatures? Then, why lay claim to singularity and *imitatio dei*? Then, why be committed, why carry the human moral load? Are we not, the mourner continues to question himself, just a band of conceited and inflated daydreamers who somehow manage to convince themselves of some imaginary superiority over the brute in the jungle?

The halakha has displayed great compassion for perplexed, suffering man, firmly held in the clutches of his archenemy—death. The halakha has never tried to gloss over the sorrowful, ugly spectacle of dying man. In spite of the fact that the halakha has indomitable faith in eternal life, in immortality and in a continued transcendental existence for all human being, it did understand like a loving sympathetic mother, man's fright and confusion when confronted with death. Therefore, the halakha has tolerated those "crazy" torturing thoughts and doubts. It did not command the mourner to disown them because they contradict the basic halakhic doctrine of man's election as the king of the universe. It permitted the mourner to have his way for a while and has ruled that the latter be relieved of all mitzvot.

"One whose dead (relative) lies before him is exempt from the recital of the Shema, and from prayer and from tefillin and from all the precepts laid down in the Torah." The Palestinian Talmud, quoted by Tosafot (*B'rakhot* 17b) derives this law from the verse in Deuteronomy 16:3: "so that you may remember the day of your departure from the land of Egypt as long as you live." The commitment accepted in Egypt is applicable to the man who is preoccupied with life and not to one who has encountered death.

What is the reason behind this law exempting the mourner from the performance of mitzvot? Because our commitment to God is rooted in the awareness of human dignity and sanctity. Once the perplexed, despairing individual begins to question whether or not such distinctiveness or choiceness exists, the whole commitment expires. Man who has faith in himself, who is aware of his charisma, was chosen and burdened with obligations and commandments. Despairing, skeptical man was not elected. How can the mourner pronounce a benediction or say "amen" if he is "speechless"? He is still capable of producing sounds, but a benediction consists of spiritual words and not of physical sounds.

In a word, the motto of *aninut* is to be found in the old pessimistic verse in the book of Ecclesiastes: "so that man has no preeminence above the beast, for all is vanity."

Avelut

At this point, the dialectical halakha which has masterfully employed both the thesis and the antithesis in her treatment of antinomies makes an about-face. The halakha was firmly convinced that man is free and that he is master not only over his deeds but over his emotions as well. The halakha held the view that man's mastery over his emotional life is unqualified, and that he is capable of changing thought patterns, emotional structures, and experimental motifs within an infinitesimal period of time.

Man, the halakha maintained, does not have to wait patiently for one mood to pass and for another to emerge gradually. He disengages himself, quickly and actively, and in a wink replaces a disjunctive frame of mind with a cathartic-redemptive one. Hence, the halakha, which showed so much tolerance for the mourner during the stage of *aninut* and let him float with the tide of black despair, now—forcefully and with a shift of emphasis—commands him that with interment (*s'timat ha-golel*) the first phase of grief come abruptly to a close and a second phase—that of *avelut*—begin.

With the commencement of *avelut*, the halakha commands the mourner to undertake an heroic task: to start picking up the debris of his own shattered personality and to reestablish himself, as man, restoring lost glory, dignity, and uniqueness. Instead of repeating to himself time and again that man has no preeminence above the beast and that all is vanity, he is suddenly told by the halakha to be mindful of the antithesis: "Thou hast chosen man at the very inception and thou hast recognized him as worthy of standing before Thee".

Yes, the halakha tells man, death is indeed something ugly and frightening, something grisly and monstrous; yes, death is trailing behind every man trying to defeat him, his ambitions, and his aspirations; all that is true. Nevertheless, the halakha adds, death must not confuse man; the latter must not plunge into total darkness because of death. On the contrary, the halakha asserts, death gives man the opportunity to display greatness and to act heroically; to build even though he knows that he will not live to enjoy the sight of the magnificent edifice in whose construction he is engaged, to plant even though he does not expect to eat the fruit, to explore, to develop, to enrich—not himself but coming generations.

Death teaches man to transcend his physical self and to identify with the timeless covenantal community. Death, the halakha warns the mourner, not only does not free man from his commitment but, on the contrary, enhances his role as a historic being and sensitizes his moral consciousness. The day is short, the workload is heavy, the Master is strict and demanding, and the commitment, therefore, is great.

While before burial, in the stage of *aninut*, man mourned in total darkness and confusion and his grief expressed itself in an act of resignation from his greatness and choiceness, after burial, in stage two, man mourns in an enlightened mood and his grief asserts itself in the awareness of human greatness and human election.

The ceremonial turning point at which *aninut* is transformed into *avelut*, despair into intelligent sadness, and self-negation into self-affirmation, is to be found in the recital of Kaddish at *s'timat ha-golel.*

The Kaddish marks the beginning of a new phase of courageous and heroic mourning to which the message of salvation is addressed. What is the relationship between the proclamation of the solemn doxology and burial? Through the Kaddish we hurl defiance at death and its fiendish conspiracy against man. When the mourner recites "Glorified and sanctified be the great name . . ." he declares more or less the following: No matter how powerful death is, notwithstanding the ugly end of man, however terrifying the grave is, however nonsensical and absurd everything appears, no matter how black one's despair is and how nauseating an affair life itself is, we declare and profess publicly and solemnly that we are not giving up, that we are not surrendering, that we will carry on the work of our ancestors as if nothing had happened, that we will not be satisfied with less than the full realization of the ultimate goal—the establishment of God's kingdom, resurrection of the dead and eternal life for man.

T'shuva in Avelut

A question arises: What is the experiential substance of *avelut*-mourning in the second phase? The latter is intrinsically an experience of *t'shuva*, repentance. The aching heart is a contrite heart, and a contrite heart is, of course, an atoning heart. Enlightened *avelut* contains a feeling of guilt. In fact, the laws concerning the observance of *shiva* express not only a mood of grieving but also, and perhaps mainly, a mood of repenting. Quite a few of the injunctions governing the observance of *shiva* (prohibitions against washing, the use of cosmetics, ointments, wearing shoes, sex life) are reminiscent of Yom Kippur. Somehow, we arrive at a strange equation: the act of mourning equals the act of expiation. The halakha commands the mourner to expiate his guilt with observing prescribed rites which are also observed on the Holy Day of Atonement when man is questing for forgiveness. What is the feeling of guilt which is implied in *avelut* and with which the halakha is concerned?

First, death per se is a consequence of sin or human imperfection. If man were perfect, if the ultimate moral law were within his reach, if he had not fallen away from his Maker, man could combat death. As a matter of fact, we do believe, as was mentioned above, that in the eschatological world, where man will attain absolute perfection, death will be finally defeated. The equation of mourning and repentance is expressed in the passage in Tractate *Moed Katan* (15b): "A mourner is bound to overturn his couch, because Bar Kappara taught: God says: I have set the likeness of my image in them, and through their sins have I upset it. Let your couches be overturned on account thereof." The passage becomes intelligible if we take into consideration that according to talmudic and midrashic symbolic semantics, the term "*mita*" (couch or bed) represents man as father and teacher, as a link between past and future both at a natural and spiritual level. If man fails to discharge his twofold duty, his image is tarnished and death follows. The overturned couch represents a desecrated image of man and the mourning rites an act of expiation.

Second, the aspect of guilt is interwoven into the human time consciousness. Man is a tragic as well as a comic figure in a variety of ways. However, his peculiar way of forming value judgments is the saddest of all his experiences and, at the same time, the most ludicrous of all his comic performances.

Man is always a latecomer as far as the formation of value judgments is concerned. His axiology or appreciation of persons, things and events is a product of hindsight.

In retrospection man discovers the precise value of something which (or somebody who) was but is no longer with us. This kind of tardiness or of being late in understanding and appreciating is, as I said above, tragic as well as comic. In fact, the comic deepens the tragic. While the somebody was near, while I could communicate with the somebody, I was unaware of him, as if he had been nobody. He comes into existence and turns into somebody very important and precious at the very instant he departs from me and is lost in the mist of remoteness. Only after he has gone I begin to ask: Who was he? What did he mean to me?

All those questions, which descend in droves upon the grieving, expiating individual, are extremely painful since they are saturated with a feeling of guilt. One torturing, cruel question stands out, namely: why didn't I ask all those questions yesterday or yesteryear while the somebody was still here? The Talmud (*B'rakhot* 42b) tells us a strange story. "Rav died. His disciples followed his bier. On their trip back home, they stopped and ate a meal by the river Danak. When they were about to say grace they become involved in a question which they could not resolve. Whereupon, Rav Adda bar Ahabah rose and made another rent in his garment which he had already torn and he said: 'Rav is dead and we have not learned even the rules about grace.'" They discovered the greatness of their master and their dependence upon him on the day on which they buried him.

How sad and how ironic! They studied under him, he trained their minds, fashioned their outlook, and opened up to them new worlds of thought, and yet he remained unknown to them. They all looked upon him as upon "the great master of the Diaspora," they all admired and revered him, and yet even they failed to see Rav's real stature and greatness until he had vanished from their midst.

This tragic as well as comic aspect of man is often the source of sin. The latter is precipitated by human harshness and insensitivity to the Divine Presence. Man does not feel the secret vigor, joy, and bliss that flow spontaneously from God's nearness. Man is unaware of God's working and acting through him while God uses him as the instrument of His will. Consequently, man sins; God departs and leaves man alone. Only then does lonely man comprehend the magnitude of his loss and nostalgically reaches for God. However, by the time man decides to turn to God, God is gone and man has nobody to turn to. All he finds then is an empty space and a mechanical, indifferent world. "From afar the Lord appeareth unto me" (Jeremiah 31:2). God becomes visible to man only from a distance, not when God wants to be really close to man. God allures and fascinates man from the infinite, uncharted lanes of the Beyond, not while God is ready to be in immediate, intimate contact with him.

Many a time the Bible, while telling us about sin, adds significantly either "and it came to pass on the morrow" or "early next morning." Only on the morrow following the night of insensitivity and hardness to God does man begin to value divine comradeship and friendship, the happiness which he could have enjoyed if he had opened up his heart to God just a few seconds prior to God's departure.

Avelut during *shiva* or *sh'loshim* is an act of atonement or expiation for human insensitivity vis-à-vis both God and fellow man.

Two Types of Teachers

We have assembled here tonight burdened with a feeling of guilt for being late in our inquiry and in asking the characteristic question. *Ilu zakhinu*, had we been deserving, we would have formulated the question long ago in the present tense: Who is he? *V'akhshav she-lo zakhinu*, since we have not been deserving, we'll ask the same question in the past tense: Who was he? Whom did we lose? His image fascinates us from afar.

At the funeral I raised this question. Of course, due to the fact that I was in a state of total confusion and despair, I could not pursue the analysis in an orderly manner. Tonight I shall undertake to complete what I could not do then and answer the nostalgic-tragic question. I said in my eulogy that my strong attachment to the Talner Rebbe and my love for him were due to a paradox, namely: the Talner Rebbe was a representative of a great and glorious tradition which has been the very antithesis of another tradition—equally glorious and great—into which I was born and on which I was reared in my ancestral home. I mentioned that all our great leaders, both ḥasidic and mitnagdic, were preoccupied with and committed to one task—teaching. The teacher, the rebbe, has been throughout the generations the central figure within the covenantal community. The teacher towered above any other figure—king, warlord, or high priest. The power which the scholar wielded was not of a political but of a spiritual nature. He never imposed his authority upon his disciples. The reverse was true. The disciples elected him and surrendered to him. I went on to say that there were two traditions of teaching, *malkhut* teaching and *k'dusha* teaching.

There was the king-teacher—"and there was a king in Jeshurun when the heads of the people were together."

Moses the greatest of all teachers, was a king in Jeshurun;
he was the king teacher. There was also the priest-teacher
or the saint-teacher—"for the priest's lips should keep
knowledge and they should seek the Law at his mouth, for
he is the messenger of the Lord of Hosts." Aaron was also a
teacher but different from Moses; he was the priest or saint-
teacher. Throughout our history, both king-teacher and saint-
teacher taught, both enlightened the minds, both molded
the characters, both propagated the word of God, both led
their respective communities along the righteous paths, both
sacrificed for and loved their communities. Nevertheless,
their methodologies, their approaches, the media they
employed were different.

King-teacher and saint-teacher were very close to each
other as far as the ultimate objective was concerned and at
the same time very remote from each other as regards
methodology, approach, and media. Let me now analyze
the basic distinctions between these two teachers.

Engaging the Mind and Touching the Soul

The king-teacher addresses himself to the mind. He teaches
both pure halakha and applied halakha. He teaches disciples
how to conceptualize, how to classify, how to reconcile
texts and opinions, how to systematize, to infer, and to
analyze. In short, he teaches them *otiyot ha-Torah*, the
mystery of combining letters into words, words into sentences,
sentences into chapters, and chapters into stories. A great
light emanates from the king-teacher. He demands clarity
and distinctness. Maimonides, the Gaon of Vilna, R. Hayyim
of Brisk represented the king-teacher tradition par excellence.
They all communicated and communed with the minds and
consequently the medium of their communication and
communion was the word. The intellect does not understand
anything but the word.

The priest or saint-teacher is also busy teaching *otiyot ha-Torah*, explaining the mystery of merging letters into words, sentences, chapters, and stories. However, while the king-teacher is concerned with visible, tangible letters, *otiyot*, with the body of the Torah, the saint-teacher focuses his attention upon the invisible, intangible letters, the soul of the Torah. The Torah, like the human being, has both—according to the Zohar—a concrete body consisting of a thought system and a moral-religious code and a soul, an overflowing inward life, which can be felt but not understood.

To feel the inner life, the mysterious heartbeat of the Torah, one has to identify himself with her and to attain unity of God's word and human existence. The task of the saint-teacher is to draw man into this kind of unity. Therefore, the saint-teacher speaks to the heart, communes with the heart and tells the heart how to attune its own excited, accelerated beat to that of the Torah. The saint-teacher teaches man the art of catharsis, how to cleanse and purge the heart of vulgarity and inhumanity, of unworthy sentiments, uncouth emotions and selfish desires, how can a man merge his soul with the soul of Torah if his inner life is unclean?

The saint-teacher teaches how a Jew should celebrate victory when the Almighty is good to him and how to experience sadness and grief when the Almighty turns His countenance away from him. Judaism has a moral code which is concerned not only with actions but with experiences as well. Many commandments in the Torah are exclusively concerned with the inner life of the Jew. The Sabbath, the holidays, represent not just a bundle of "don'ts"—thou shall not—but a great, redeeming, experiential reality. What is prayer if not worship by the heart? And what is *Shema* if not an act of inner surrender? It is obvious that experiences leading to merger and unity with the Torah and, through it, with God cannot be taught by the loud word which represents the logos.

How can the saint-teacher tell his disciples what he experiences on Yom Kippur during the recital of the *Avoda* when his soul migrates to the Temple of ancient Jerusalem and joins the high priest on his way to the Holy of Holies. Experiences resist objectification by the logos-word. They cannot be pressed into sound. They are too fluid, too amorphous and too subjective! Experiences are handed down through the silent word, not taught through the loud word. One communicates an experience the way a sick person communicates a disease. Experiences are indeed contagious like infectious diseases. One catches a disease by being in contact with a sick person. One also catches an experience by being in contact with the saint-teacher who is lovesick.

Teaching the Few and Reaching the Many

The king-teacher is engaged in an esoteric gesture, for any kind of teaching, religious or secular, is an esoteric performance limited to a small group of talented people or to an intellectual elite. One cannot convert a whole nation into scholars. Only in the messianic era does Isaiah (54:13) foresee universal scholarship: "and all thy children shall be taught of the Lord." Not everybody is capable of understanding an abstract scientific or halakhic system, let alone of contributing to it. The king-teacher must satisfy himself with a limited group of the bright and talented, with the select few.

In contrast, the saint-teacher addresses himself to the entire community. He does not discriminate between the bright and the dull. Not all Jews are intellectual geniuses, but they all have sensitive hearts; they all quest for God; they all want to feel Him, to experience Him; they all are overcome by a strong passion for *k'dusha.* Every Jew, *ḥasidut* taught, is capable of finding God if he is earnest in his search and quest. "But from thence ye will seek the Lord thy God; and thou shalt find Him if thou search after Him with all thy heart and with all thy soul." Hence the teaching of the saint-teacher is exoteric, democratic, understandable and accessible to both the simpleton and philosopher.

As a matter of fact, if we should examine the ḥasidic movement, we shall find that not all of its teachers and leaders chose to be saint-teachers whose job it is to teach the crowd, the privileged and the underprivileged. Quite a few of the ḥasidic great preferred the king-teacher—"and there was a king in Jeshurun" tradition—to the saint-teacher—"for the priest's lips should keep knowledge" tradition. Those teachers intellectualized *ḥasidut*, emphasizing the role of the scholastic community and its intellectual attainments. Ḥabad has restored esotericism; so did the school of Kotzk, which left an indelible mark upon Polish ḥasidism. It is enough to mention just the names Ger, Sochochov, and Radzin in order to realize the extent of this change. Only the *ḥasidut* of Tchernobil dynasty, founded by Rabbi Naḥum of Tchernobil, refused to change roles and has steadfastly clung to the tradition of saint-teacher, whom they called "*maggid*." They kept on teaching everyone who was hungry for knowledge and thirsty for God's word.

Ḥesed and Emet

The king-teacher and the saint-teacher differ also in another respect: their solutions to the *ḥesed-emet* dialectic are not identical, even though the difference is more a matter of emphasis than of substance.

Let us see what the dialectic consists of. What is *ḥesed* if not unconditional compassion and unreserved kindness. The very essence of *ḥesed* expresses itself in its universality, in its ultimate love from which no one is excluded, in its great sympathy, encompassing every human being in its all-embracing and all inclusive concern. The *ish ḥesed*, the person of *ḥesed*, does not ask the recipient of his love to present moral credentials. He does not demand in exchange for his love a meritorious performance or a great accomplishment. His love is gratuitous as well as boundless.

What is *emet* if not strict, unbending justice and ultimate truth ? In the eyes of the *ish emet*, the person of truth, nothing must be given gratuitously. One must be rewarded in accordance with his merits. If a person is deserving, he should be loved. If he is not deserving, love should be denied to him. Any deviation is unpardonable. The slightest inconsistency is unforgivable. The sinner, the evildoer, must not be loved. Hence, love from the standpoint of *emet* cannot be universal. To speak of undeserved love is an infraction of the *emet* norm. How should man decide? How is he supposed to act vis-à-vis this controversy? Man faces the challenge either to be all-loving and betray truth or to be absolutely truthful and love only some people. Medieval man sinned by ignoring *ḥesed* and choosing *emet*—whatever he thought to be true—as his single guiding principle. Modern man, in reverse, chose *ḥesed* as his lodestar.

Medieval man was a zealot, a fanatic; modern man is a compromiser. Our Torah has devoted considerable attention to the problem of reconciliation of both opposites. It is self-evident that ultimate reconciliation can only be found in God; man may find only a relative solution to the problem, depending upon the temperament and outlook of the person. At this juncture, the king-teacher and saint-teacher part. They both have discovered a formula how to harmonize *ḥesed* and *emet*. However, while the king-teacher places the emphasis upon *emet*, the saint-teacher stresses *ḥesed*. They both love, and both are committed to the truth. And yet they act differently.

The king-teacher rebukes the sinner in harsh words. The saint-teacher just sheds a tear when he encounters sin. The king-teacher scorns iniquity loudly. The saint-teacher is saddened by iniquity—but he remains silent. The king-teacher shows anger at the sight of injustice. The saint-teacher displays childish amazement when confronted with injustice. The king-teacher fights for *emet* by demonstrating strength and boldness, the saint–teacher by reproaching the sinner the way a loving mother reproaches a mischievous child. The sermon of king-teacher is a loud one, saturated with a prophetic anger. The sermon of the saint-teacher is a silent one, saturated with prophetic love: "The law of truth was in his mouth . . . He walked with Me in peace and uprightness."

There are two images of man: the projected public image and the hidden, private image. Man, on the one hand, is a social being; he is gregarious, fond of company, living within a group. On the other hand, man is an individual; a lonely being. He lives always in retreat; he is reticent and shy, unwilling to disclose his inner thoughts to, or confide in, others. He does not want people to see him crying or watch him dancing. He hides in the shadows. We do speak of *homo kevelatus*, known man, and *homo absconditus*, man in hiding, man-mystery. This dual aspect of man is a result of his being created in the image of God, who sometimes reveals Himself to us through the cosmic process and at other times hides Himself behind this very cosmic process. We sanctify God by saying "the fullness of all the earth is His glory." We also sanctify Him by saying "Blessed is the Lord from His abode of transcendental mystery and unknowability." Quite often, he is *deus revelatus*, and frequently He is *deus absconditus*: "and God descended in the cloud."

The king-teacher is mainly a *homo revelatus*. Teaching through the word is an act of revelation. The saint-teacher

reveals very little of himself. He is unknown, no matter how
many admire him. He leads a secluded, silent, lonely existence,
even though his message is addressed to many. He teaches
the multitude, but only few know him. He loves many, he
has compassion with many, but only a limited group
understands him.

The Talner Rebbe

Who was the Talner Rebbe? He was the saint-teacher par
excellence. He represented with great dignity and sacrificial
action six generations of saint-teachers, the great *maggidim*.
He personified the *ḥesed* tradition of the Tchernobiler *maggid*
with dedication and sincerity. I never saw him alone. I
always saw him in company: R. David of Talne on his right
and R. Naḥum of Tchernobil on his left. He bore such a
striking resemblance to his great-grandfather, I always felt
as if his illustrious ancestors were protecting their saintly
great-grandson, who was so humble, so shy, so honest, so
gentle, and so kind, from the vicissitudes of the cold,
insensitive world of today. He epitomized to me the great
message of the saint-teacher, the message of universal love
and unlimited truth, of being close to God and feeling His
presence. We have lost him and with him the great *maggidim*
and saint-teachers disappeared from our midst. A terrible
void was left and a great dreariness. I feel kind of lonely
without him. I look at the empty chair and quite often I am
tempted to kiss the place whereupon the Talner Rebbe sat
and say what R. Joshua ben Ḥananiah said when he kissed
the stone on which R. Eliezer the great sat: "This stone is
like Mount Sinai, and the person who sat on it is like the
Ark of the Covenant."

Jews at Prayer

The following essay contains the Rav's personal reflections on prayer and an evaluation of contemporary formats for prayer.

Judaism has always grasped *t'filla* as a "worship of the heart" (*avoda she-balev*), a heart, quick-throbbing and disorderly, overflowing with desire of the divine, full of yearning and wonder and dissonance, a heart so "mad," so "wild," so "primitive" that it almost fears to cross the threshold of the "Temple" where everything is orderly and cultured and suffused with rationality. The magnificent Jewish heart prayed and tendered prayer from the time of Abraham and on. From a musical viewpoint the forms developed by the generations lack perfect structure. The Jewish melodic formula is often marked by the absence of strict form, and by sudden leaps and bounds. One who seeks harmonies and euphonies in the tunes of Jewish prayer is destined to disappointment. What can be found is stichic eruption of feeling. For example, hope and vision in *"Uv'khen ten pahd'kha"*, quiet joy and yearning in *"Ha-kohanim v'ha-am"*, the despair and sorrow of *"Ashamnu"* or *"Ana Ha-Shem,"* melancholy combined with uplifting as in the Kaddish of *Ne'ila*, solemnity and tension as in Kol Nidrei. None of these tunes bursts into tone-rich song, but rather are a flowing of heartfelt feelings and soulfulness, the voice of *"Min ha-Metzar," "Mima'amakim," "T'filla le-Ani"*. This is the music of worship of the heart in which form is drowned in content, prose in feeling, the external in the inward. The heart—the truth—reacts.

I imagine a *Kol Nidrei* night in the *Bet Midrash* of the Baal Shem Tov or the Tanya *z"l*. They did not use "music," choirs, or glorified tunes and pompous song. They certainly had no carpeted platforms, flowers, or "rabbis" trained in elocution and etiquette; the simplest of Jews prayed there, who were as far as can be from the aesthetics of Yefet, but who were scions of an ancient root, indispensable links in the chain of generations, and within whom the fire of faith burned: "Intense as death is love . . ." Form was totally lacking, but for that reason there blazed upward a storm of faith, a tremendous love and desire for the Creator. The worshippers must have all swayed like trees in a forest swept by a hurricane.

I think I have the right to describe such a scene, for in my own childhood memories, half enwrapped in mist and half romanticized, I can still see the vigorous swaying of the Ḥabad congregation on the first night of Rosh Hashana, "Coronation Night" (as the old ḥasidim called it), when lowly man, who is today here and tomorrow in the grave, offers the royal crown to the Ancient of Days, to the Infinite, to the Everliving, when man calls Him Holy King (*Ha-Melekh Ha-Kadosh*). I can still hear the low hum of hundreds of Jews, spiritually on fire, passing through the shul as the *ḥazzan* finished Kaddish and the congregants began the Amida, the sound of something sublime and lofty, aflame and alive, something that did not need cantor or choir or theatricalities in order to reach the Gates of Heaven.

Does the fountain, leaping from the ground in all its primal force, need any artificial setting to give it majesty and impressiveness? Must lava eructated by the burning volcano move in time with the rules of some hollow decorum? It is precisely in their naturalness, their spontaneity, that their beauty is revealed. And is not man attempting to pray a leaping fountain or even a fire-spitting mountain?

Clearly, prayer is the opposite of ceremony with regard to the relation of form and content, heart and word. If so, then all those aesthetic reforms in prayer will, instead of deepening the experience, rob it of its content and soul.

Other characteristics of ceremonialism are also alien to service of the heart. If true prayer takes place in the heart one does not need a master of ceremonies to mediate between the congregation and the Creator. Judaism teaches that every individual possesses a heart full of love—conscious or unconscious—for God; his heart is as near to the Gates of Heaven as that of the "clergyman," often more so. There is no need for the "rabbi" to stand on a pulpit, adorned with the "priestly vestments," to stage the prayers. He and the simple Jew have exactly the same status before God. And they can both pray on the same synagogue floor. I do not intend to get involved in the halakhic details relating to the prohibition of standing on a platform when one prays; one thing I know—that standing in a place more elevated than that where the rest of the people are standing contradicts "service of the heart," which is an expression of "Out of the depths." The counterfeit role of the "rabbi" in the conduction of prayer stems from the false concept of ceremoniality that has penetrated our thinking about prayer.

Above all, one cannot separate service of the heart from life. When man stands before his Creator he must give an accounting of all his quotidian activities outside the synagogue. Prayer must be a mirror of human behavior; it should never become a power force enabling one to escape from oneself and from one's moral obligations. Unlike the churches, Jewish synagogues never developed architectonic or decorative means with which to enchant man, to anesthetize him into a supernatural mood. They never created the illusion of standing before God when the heart seeks Him not, when the heart is, in fact, hard as stone, cruel and cynical. Our synagogues were never in the dominion of half-darkness; the clear light of the sun was never hidden by narrow stained glass windows. There never echoed the rich, polyphonic strains of the organ, and the song of the mixed choir, hidden from the eyes of worshippers, in order to create a mysterious, unworldly mood. They never tried to extract the Jew from reality, to introduce him to spirits. To the contrary: they always demanded that prayer be continuous to life and that in it man confess the truth. For this reason the Catholic-style dramatization of prayer is so utterly alien to our religious sense; therefore the great opposition of halakha to so-called modernization of prayer services which erases the uniquely original in "worship of the heart."

Sh'ḥora Ani V'nava

"Sh'ḥora Ani V'nava" concerns itself with the dialectical predicates of repentance. It is part of a larger Yiddish lecture called *B'rit Avot* (The Ancestral Covenant), which was delivered by the Rav at a conference of the Religious Zionists of America.

> When thou hast made an end of tithing all the tithe of thine increase in the third year, the year of tithing, and hast given unto the Levite, to the stranger, to the fatherless and to the widow, that they may eat within thy gates, and be satisfied. Then thou shalt say before the Lord thy God: "I have put away the hallowed things out of my house, and have also given it unto the Levite, and unto the stranger, to the fatherless, and to the widow, according to all Thy commandment which Thou hast commanded me; I have not transgressed any of Thy commandments, neither have I forgotten. I have not eaten thereof in my mourning; neither have I put away thereof, being unclean, nor given thereof for the dead; I have hearkened to the voice of the Lord my God, I have done according to all that Thou hast commanded me (Deuteronomy 26:12–14).

This portion is recited by a Jew twice in the *Sh'mitta* cycle, in the fourth and the seventh years, when he completes the *Seder ha-ma'asrot.* (There is a controversy between the Rambam and the Raavad if the recitation of this portion must necessarily take place in the Bet ha-Mikdash.)

One thing draws our attention, namely: a halakhic term. The mishnayot in *Ma'aser Sheni* and *Sota*, and the Talmud in many instances, designate the recital of the portion—"I have put away the hallowed things out of my house"—the *ma'aser* "confession" (*vidui ma'aser*). Mishna 7:1 in *Sota*

86

says: "The following are recited in any language: the *sota* portion, the *ma'aser* 'confession' (*vidui ma'aser*), and *k'riat Shema* . . ." Mishna 5:10 in *Ma'aser Sheni* employs the same terms: "In *minḥa* on the last holiday they would 'confess.' What was the form of the 'confession'? . . ." The terms appear also in mishnayot 5:11, 12, and 14: "Then, if one (gave) *ma'aser sheni* prior to (*ma'aser*) *rishon* he may not 'confess'"; "Then, if one ate while in the state of *aninut*, one may not 'confess'"; and "From this source they said: Israelites and *mamzerim* may 'confess' . . ." As a rule, in all sources recital of the *parasha* is thought of as "confession" (*vidui*).

Prima facie, the title "Confession" is not fitting for this *parasha*. We know what confession stands for: We confess that we have sinned, transgressed, erred. We all know what the Yom Kippur confession means (both the abbreviated confession—"However we and our ancestors have sinned," and the extended confession—"For the sin"): an act of merciless accusation and self-condemnation. However, in the *ma'aser* portion there is no account of sins, but to the contrary: of mitzvot and good deeds. The Jew boasts that he has not violated even one order and that he has fulfilled the mitzva of *ma'asrot* to the letter: "according to all Thy commandment which Thou hast commanded me: I have not transgressed any of Thy commandments, neither have I forgotten. . . . I have hearkened to the voice of the Lord my God, I have done according to all that Thou hast commanded me." The Talmud in *Sota* equates the *ma'aser* portion with the voicing of man's praise. How, then, have our Sages *z"l* endowed the recital of the portion with the title of "Confession?" What type of confession is this? How can the praise of man simultaneously be the confession of man?

In this nomenclature lies encouched a basic principle of Jewish thinking regarding repentance and confession.

Repentance is predicated on two principles:

1. On the power within men to be able to accuse themselves, on their ability to think of themselves as unworthy and inferior. In our declaration on Yom Kippur "And You are justified for all that befalls us, for You have acted correctly and we have acted evilly," emerges the expression of that wonderful power of full, boundless self-accusation.

2. On the great talent of each individual to cleanse himself, to comprehend the boundless hidden spiritual powers, which are found in the human personality (including even the greatest sinner) and which propel one in the direction of return to the Sovereign of the universe; on the ability of men to ascend and to elevate themselves to the majestic heights, if only one has the will to do so, even after he has sunk to the depths of the abyss of impurity.

The second principle is just as important as the first. A man, obviously, cannot engage in repentance if he does not have the boldness to accuse and condemn. Without recognition of the sin there can be no regret. On the other hand, however, we cannot imagine recognition of sin and a commitment for the future if the man has no faith in his own creative abilities and if he does not believe in his own talents which will aid him to sanctify himself. If he believes that he is helpless and, therefore, subservient to natural, mechanical powers, if he is not convinced of the freedom of the human creative act—then he cannot feel his guilt and there is no basis to expect that he will change. Within the greatness of man lies contained the greatest accusative act and from it comes the call to repentance. If man looks upon himself as an impotent creature then the position of the sinner is helpless. And then the plea of Jews "For our crimes and our transgressions are upon us, and in them we decay" becomes warranted.

Every confession expresses itself in the outcry: "I am

black and I am beautiful, O daughters of Jerusalem." When
we do not see the "Beauty" we cannot discern the "Blackness".
There is no distinction whether we cry out: "I am black and
I am beautiful," or "I am beautiful and I am black." All that
is important is that the sinner view himself from two antithetical
viewpoints, the nullity of being and the greatness of being.
Thus, the praise of man, just as his shame, is a part of
confession. Thus, the portion "I have hearkened to the
voice of the Lord my God, I have done according to all that
Thou hast commanded me" is considered a "confession."
Man declares through the recital of the portion that he is
able to live, in accord with the will of the Sovereign of the
Universe, a life of sanctity and purity. If he has manifested
his power to fulfill the will of the Holy One Blessed Be He
in many difficult situations, then we have a right to demand
of him, that he shall demonstrate this strength under all
circumstances. The consequence is that he who says "I have
done according to all that Thou hast commanded me" is
responsible for errors with regard to many things, where he
has neglected his duty and where he has acted like "blackness"
and not like "beauty." If he stands fast with pride, saying "I
have done according to all that Thou hast commanded me,"
he will also be able to admit with humbleness, "I have not
done according to all that Thou hast commanded me."

How beautiful is Rashi's account in the name of the midrash
on the verse "'And he made the laver of brass, and the base
thereof of brass, from the mirrors of the serving women . . .'[1]—The daughters of Israel had in their possession
mirrors into which they looked when they adorned themselves
. . . But Moses was displeased with them for they were
made for the Evil Inclination. So the Holy One Blessed Be
He said to him: 'Accept, for these are more beloved by Me
than everything else . . .'" Moses did not understand how
the very mirror that the women used to employ while they

ornamented themselves for their husbands and while they
gained pleasure from their own beauty could be properly
incorporated in the laver adjacent to the altar where a Jew
brings his sacrifice of atonement and on which he recites
confession with a broken heart. How can the beauty of the
mirrors harmonize with the sensation of blackness with
which the road to the altar is bound? However, the Sovereign
of the Universe said: "Accept, Moses!" The woman who
knows she is beautiful, who was able in Egypt, in the bitter
and dark exile, to comfort and strengthen her husband and
to raise a generation thirsty for redemption, that same woman,
when she shall transgress, will recite her confession with
hot tears and with more grief and regret than another person.
This woman will remember what she suffered in Egypt
"*taḥat ha-tapu'aḥ*"[2] and the guilt feeling will be increasingly
impressed upon her conscience.

NOTES

1. Exodus 38:8.
2. Song of Songs 8:5. See *Sota* 11b which interprets the
phrase to refer to the exile in Egypt.

Torah and Humility

A large crowd of students, faculty and alumni gather to hear the Rav's annual Yahrzeit lecture. The following lecture, entitled "Torah and Humility" was delivered on March 5, 1971.

It is quite obvious that the topic of Torah and humility is very relevant today, when the explosion of knowledge can and does lead to man's increased arrogance.

Through His word, God created the natural cosmos. The order of Creation led to scientific order. The word of God is truth and, therefore, so are the sciences. The word of God created man's freedom and the covenant between God and Abraham. The word is *k'dusha*, sanctity. We know that halakha distinguishes between objects that are intrinsically sacred and objects that are related to *k'dusha*, but are not in themselves sacred. How do we define these two categories?

The appearance of the letters of words of God always signify sanctity. That is why the *t'fillin* boxes are considered holy, while the leather straps, having no letters on them, are only related to holiness. The mere presence of letters makes the plain boxes sacred.

The source of this holiness is the Torah. Whenever the letters appear, the Torah appears, and we find inherent sanctity.

Yet Judaism has a Written Law and an Oral Law. The Written Law has inherent holiness because it has the visible, concrete words of God. But the study of the Oral Law is a thought process, not one conducted in writing. The Oral Law, therefore, transmits its sanctity in a more subtle manner. It sanctifies the human mind which is involved in its study and purifies the mind of irrelevant and meaningless thought. It adds a new dimension to the human experience—sanctity.

The term "writing" does not only include the formation of phonetic sounds. While a scribe writes the Torah on parchment, the rebbe "writes" ideas on the hearts and minds of sensitive human beings. The sanctity of the Torah is often compared to Israel—the Oral Law. The Talmud in Tractate *Sota* refers to Moses as "the great scribe of Israel." Moses was so called not because he wrote well, not because he had a nice handwriting, but rather because he passed the words and ideas of God on to the people of Israel. The *Sefer Y'tzira* also calls the Almighty a scribe and says He created the world with a scroll.

Moses, the great scribe, transmitted this to the people. The equation we thus have is writer=creation=education. A teacher is a collaborator in shaping the world.

Only human closeness to God can generate sanctity. How can one be in the proximity of God? Can one share in God's holiness? Yes, says the Talmud, by cleaving to our sages. Only through Torah can sanctity be attained.

How does Torah unite us with infinity? The *Baal ha-Tanya* invokes the principle of *aḥdut ha-maskil v'ha-muskal*: the knower and the object being known are united. If the knower and the knowable object merge into one, then if two knowers concentrate on one thing, they will be united. If a=b and c=b, then a=c. Whenever there is unity of thought and purpose, there is also personalized unity. Rambam says (in his introduction to *Avot*) that friendship is a result of the unification of minds and hearts. If identity of thought results in friendship, the same is true between man and God. If man thinks about the ideas expounded in the word of God, a similar affectionate relationship develops between man and God. As the *Tanya* says, when someone understands a halakha, "he grasps the wisdom of the Omnipresent."

Through this revelation, the divine thought was made understandable to man. The problem which now arises, however, is that this knowledge is accessible only to a select few, while the masses will never receive it. If so, how do the ignorant unite with God? Are they deprived of God's companionship because they can't carry on this intellectual process? But another doctrine exists, that of *aḥdut ha-ohev v'ha-ahuv*: the unity of the lover and the beloved. Genuine love is an identification between two people, the sharing of common destiny and goals. If so, two persons will be bound in love by their mutual love of a third person. The love of husband and wife, originally an erotic love, changes to a more sincere, spiritual love, after the birth of a first child. "And he is attached to his wife and they are one flesh." Rashi says that the child is formed by both parents, and in this manner they are one flesh. When Leah, after giving birth to Reuven said, "and now my husband will love me," she meant that what she failed to offer, her son would now offer. So too, God loves the Torah, as if it were his daughter. And we are the children of Torah. The fact that man and God share the same love of Torah unites us all. In this bond, all are children of Torah, all who support her and feel awed by her, not only those who study her. Hence the entire Jewish community is a Torah community, and therefore a holy one. Ḥasidism has always asserted that Torah is for all, not reserved only for those who learn. For this reason, it was popular with the masses.

Knowledge contributes little to the humility of man. Usually, the greater the achievement, the greater the arrogance. But Torah demands humility, since it awakens sanctity in us. How can sanctity awaken humility? Sanctity should be associated with man's greatness, his privilege of facing God. How does this feeling of sanctity result in humility, remoteness from God? The bridge is the awareness of defeat. Sanctity longs for infinity, for vastness, but the yearning for God is never satisfied, and perfect unity is impossible. The Song of

Songs describes this continual search for the impossible remoteness. "Who shall climb the mountain of God . . ." Man tries to climb the mountain but he never reaches the peak. The drive is never terminated until man is defeated. Every man, no matter how powerful he is, must experience frustration in life, and usually in the battle he wants to win most. Even Moses was defeated and did not enter the Promised Land. Why was this desire denied? Why was it one he wanted so much? Had Moses entered the land, the Temple would never have been destroyed. Moses would have ushered in the messianic era, would have captured the "crown" of the Messiah. He would have reached the peak, and nothing but inactivity would have been in store for the future of man. So Moses was defeated.

We may now see how sanctity and humility merge. Sanctity states that one is near God because he is good. Awareness says man wants to be closer to God, to merge completely, but this is impossible, because man is small.

The awareness of defeat leads to humility, which involves five aspects. The first is a knowledge of dependence. When a wise man realizes he is dependent on someone who has achieved a little more, who is wiser, who is more successful in his drive for sanctity, this leads to humility. When Korah said that "the entire people is sanctified, and God is in their midst" he was correct. Every Jew has a share in Torah. But he erred in questioning Moses' leadership. He believed that since everyone was sanctified, Moses was not needed as rebbe. But the reverse is true. The more sanctity one has, the more he needs a rebbe. This awareness of dependence is expressed through gratitude and loyalty. The proud person can't admit that his accomplishments are due to other people. Judaism believes that no man is self-sufficient. Naval ha-Carmeli (in Samuel I) was an egotist, feeling that he alone was master of his own destiny. He felt that he owed nothing to anyone. But this approach is contrary to Judaism, since humble man is indebted to fellow man. Why does the Torah deal with the story of Lot in such great detail? What was his contribution to us? The reason is that Abraham was committed to Lot, as Abraham's central virtues were loyalty and gratitude. The Torah speaks so much of Lot because Abraham displayed great loyalty to him. Our sages say that when Abraham told the Egyptians that Sara was his sister, Lot restrained himself from revealing their secret. Thus Abraham never forgot the favor.

Intellectual caution is another step to humility. A humble student is careful in rendering halakhic decisions and does not proclaim high-sounding theories.

A third facet is ethical modesty. One must be modest in his self-evaluation and must be aware of his inadequacy.

The fourth step is retreat. The same wise man who hungers for sanctity and wisdom is quite often capable of limitation. He is disciplined and self-controlled, and possesses the ability to retreat. Rambam (in *Hilkhot Dei'ot*) says that there is physiological retreat by controlling one's appetite, and there is also social retreat, by not attracting attention. A wise man must dress appropriately in order not to attract attention. He must contain his emotions as well. When he succeeds, he praises God for his success but he does not brag and boast to others. "And Haman described the extent of his wealth"—he boasted. The more retreat one has, the less the external world knows of his success. If someone is in distress, let him pray to God but not cry aloud, become hysterical, and lose one's dignity. The greater the wise man, the greater he must limit his emotions. It is every man's duty to spread Torah to others. Thought eventually is expressed, but emotions must not be displayed. Here is where retreat must be applied.

The final step is generosity. This denotes that one is dependent upon others and others dependent on him.

Rambam (in *Guide to the Perplexed*) says that generosity is embracing a friend as a part of oneself. It is a desire of generosity to be loved and to want to give love. On the sentence "*V'Ḥanah m'daberet al libah*" (And Ḥanah was speaking of her heart), the Talmud (in *B'rakhot*) says she wanted someone on whom she could center and focus all her love. Prophetic messages, too, cannot be kept within—"And the word of God was as a fire within me," said Jeremiah. He had to say the prophecy. The wise man must realize that not only are there people above him but there are people below who require his teachings. The sages say that God teaches little children who die before they receive an education. If so, we can do the same. But generosity also denotes faith in the above. Without this faith, no motive for generosity could exist. The wise man must believe in the people, in the congregation as a whole. The Torah has guaranteed that the Children of Israel will repent. Every Jew has the capacity for repentance, and nobody is to be expelled.

The First Rebellion
against Torah Authority

What follows is a reconstruction from prepared notes of a lecture given by Rabbi Soloveitchik at the 19th Annual R.C.A. Convention.

In explaining the rebellion of Koraḥ, one must analyze the two main arguments he employed (as indicated in the Torah and in the Midrash) and thereby gain insight into his personal motivations and the ideology he proclaimed. What will emerge from this analysis are insights into challenges to Torah authority at all times, including our own. Contemporary attempts to reinterpret halakha or to reject it outright are but echoes of what transpired in the days of Moses.

Prior to Koraḥ we find many complaints on the part of the People of Israel, prompted by understandable needs and fears, but never a rebellion. Given the frightening conditions of desert life and the consequent exaggerated emotional extremes it induces (see Numbers 13:28) their complaints are almost to be expected. Some examples of grievances prior to Koraḥ's rebellion include fear of the pursuing Egyptians (Exodus 14:10), thirst (Exodus 15:24 and 17:2,3), and hunger (Exodus 16:2,3).

In addition, there was the sin of the golden calf (Exodus 32). But even that grave violation was not precipitated by idolatrous ideas or philosophical doubts. Rather it was motivated by primitive instinctive fears which would understandably emerge in that arid wilderness (note the commentaries). Moses had not returned on the calculated day and the people felt leaderless. They felt like a lost sheep which had strayed from its shepherd and flocks. Quite understandably they sought some tangible symbol of

security to replace Moses. This is explicit in the words of
the text (Exodus 32:1). Thus, none of the above are to be
categorized as rebellions.

Koraḥ's defiance of Moses, however, was for the first time
a planned conspiracy, initiated by a small group of elite
individuals who were prompted by a lust for power.
Demagogic means to arouse the masses were employed.
Dissidents and malcontents with previous grievances (for
example, members of the tribe of Reuven) were drawn in.
Their goal was to topple Moses from his position of leadership.
A new ideology based on the presumption of greater
democracy, and on more logical halakha was formulated.
No petty quarrel, desert fears, or sudden ungratified needs
prompted this rebellion. This was no spontaneous outburst
of the masses. From the very outset it was a conspiracy for
power.

According to Ramban, Koraḥ's enmity began when Aaron
was elevated to the High Priesthood and the Levites were
derogated to being mere assistants of the *kohanim* (the
priests). Although this had happened a year earlier, Koraḥ
did not dare to publicly come out against Moses then because
the masses adored him. "They [the masses] loved him [Moses]
as [they loved] their own lives . . . and had any man defied
Moses at that time, the people would have stoned him"
(Naḥmanides, Commentary on the Torah). Koraḥ therefore
bided his time, waiting for the moment when Moses' authority
would be undermined. *Rishonim* argue as to when the
rebellion occurred.

Ibn Ezra places it after the completion of the *Mishkan*
(Tabernacle). Naḥmanides, however, insists that it followed
the episode of the *miraglim*. First, he argues, there is no
reason to disturb the textual chronology unless absolutely
compelled to do so. Second, Datan and Aviram's reply to
Moses, sarcastically referring to Egypt as "flowing with milk

and honey" and accusing him of "committing us to death in the desert" (Numbers 16:13), logically follows the *miraglim* decree.

This was the propitious moment Koraḥ had been waiting for. God's severe punishment and Moses' inability to undo the decree were a shock to the people. While they were slaves Moses had promised to take them to a land "flowing with milk and honey." Suddenly, thirty-nine more years of desert wandering was their lot. *"V'haveiti"* (Exodus 6:8) would remain unfulfilled. And they were already at the tip of the Negev, so very close to fulfillment![1] Moses' helplessness reduced his popularity to a very low ebb. At this moment of despair and disillusionment Koraḥ made his move.

The story of Koraḥ's rebellion begins with the enigmatic phrase *"va-yikaḥ Koraḥ"* (literally, "Koraḥ took"; Numbers 16:1). Rashi's two explanations suggest an enlargement of the conspiracy from his personal grievance to the formation of an anti-Moses movement. "He took himself to one side in order to separate himself from the community in order to raise a protest concerning the priestly appointment . . . Another explanation of 'Koraḥ took': he attracted [won over] the heads of Sanhedrin from amongst them [the people] by words [cogent arguments]."

Koraḥ was an intelligent man (see Rashi on Numbers 16:7), and he initiated a campaign of cajolery, persuasion, flattery, and sarcasm. At times he posed as the champion of justice (see the story of the widow in the *Midrash Tanḥuma*), and at times as the exemplar of common sense against the illogical decisions of Moses (the story of the all-blue *talitot*).

The word *"va-yikaḥ"* suggests a complete dedication to a task, a total personal commitment even to the point of self-endangerment. Naḥmanides says it connotes a mental resolve. But logistical motivations aside, every rebellion requires an ideology to arouse the fervor of the masses and to sustain its momentum. A private quarrel or particular complaint has no such need. A movement, however, needs a slogan, a motto. It must present a cause, an ideal, some higher value to be pursued, something to replace the intolerable status quo. Koraḥ advanced two ideological arguments, one found in the Torah text, and the other related by *Ḥazal*.

Koraḥ's First Argument

Simply stated, Koraḥ's first argument was "By what right may any Jew—even Moses—assume leadership and power over fellow Jews?" Koraḥ's major accusation against Moses was his (Moses') illegitimate presumption of power. Every Jew, argued Koraḥ, was equally chosen by God and consequently the intrinsic sanctity of every individual Jew, be he the great Moses or a lowly woodchopper, is equal.

"And they assembled against Moses and Aaron and said unto them, 'You have taken too much, for the entire congregation are all holy and God is in their midst, so why should you raise yourselves above God's assembly?'"

The key challenge is "Why should you raise yourselves above God's assembly," a challenge to the presumption of Moses and Aaron to authority—to rule, to judge, and to lead. Koraḥ raised a basic Jeffersonian, egalitarian, principle of democracy, stating not that all men are created equal, but that all Jews are chosen equal. Clearly this is a fundamental challenge to all authority and to all presumptions to power.

Apparently Koraḥ was unaware of the double aspect of *b'ḥira*. In Deuteronomy 14:2 we read "For you are a holy nation unto the Lord your God, and God has chosen you (*baḥar*) to be unto Him a unique nation from amongst all the nations that are on the face of the earth." Since the verse already indicated that we are "a holy nation," Rashi is troubled by the need for the subsequent phrase "and God has chosen you." He therefore states: "'You are a holy nation.—your own holiness comes to you from your fathers and in addition 'God has chosen you.'" Rashi thereby stresses that there is a double statement being made about *b'ḥira* because *b'ḥira* has a dual nature.

The two aspects of *b'ḥira* may be described as the social aspect of *k'dusha* and the individual aspect of *k'dusha*. The social aspect of *k'dusha*—the chosenness of the nation of Israel (*b'ḥirat Am Yisrael*)—means that each individual Jew possesses *k'dusha* because he is a member of the Jewish community. This communal *k'dusha* is inherited from the Patriarchs by every child born of a Jewish mother. This "spiritually genetic" *k'dusha* dates from the time of the covenants with Abraham (*b'rit bein ha-b'tarim*) and the Sinaitic covenant. The collective body—*K'nesset Yisrael*—was consecrated as a whole, and each individual draws his consecration from membership in that body, the parts reflecting the character of the whole. The word "*am*" (nation) as in *am kadosh* (a sanctified nation) is etymologically the same as *im* (together). *Am kadosh* thus implies a togetherness—holiness. It is "your own holiness [which] comes to you from your fathers."

If every Jew derives his *k'dusha* from membership in *K'nesset Yisrael*, that is, from the Patriarchs, then Moses has the same status as the lowly woodchopper. Irrespective of personal uniqueness, each individual is a passive recipient of an equal amount of sanctity. This is a democratic concept. Koraḥ's argument "Why should you raise yourselves above God's assembly?" would seem to be legitimate and morally appealing.

However, there is a second aspect to *k'dusha, k'dushat ha-yaḥid* (individual sanctity), and a second source of *k'dusha, b'ḥirat ha-yaḥid* (individual chosenness). The implication of this concept is that the individual Jew is the direct recipient of *k'dusha* according to his own unique personal endowments, efforts, and achievements. "God has chosen you." While the social aspect of *k'dusha* suppresses genius and uniqueness, making all individuals alike, *b'hirat ha-yahid* adds a personalistic element, a sanctification specific to the individual and unlike that found in anyone else. *Uv'kha bahar* ("God had chosen you") is followed by *lihiyot Lo l'am segula*; "*lihiyot*" is a challenge "to become," "to form," "to organize and bring into being the unique nation." Korah only understood the social aspect of *k'dusha*, hence he continually emphasized the congregation (*eida*) in his argument. Moses, in his rebuttal, however, does not mention the congregation but refers instead to individual chosenness. In such a context the individual does indeed rise to positions of teaching and authority according to his merits. Thus Moses' elevation is justified.

Medieval exegetes agree that the word "*boker*" (morning) is from the root "*baker*" which means to discriminate, to differentiate.[2] In contrast, the word "*erev*" (evening) connotes a period of monotonous sameness, a dulling of differentiation, a time when all forms and distinctions recede, resulting in a *ta'arovet*, a colorless mixture.

Moses said to Korah, your ideology is like *erev*. As part of the larger *eida*, all individuals lose their distinctiveness; all are alike. However, added Moses, "*Boker v'yoda Ha-Shem*," in the morning God will make known whom He has singled out and chosen. The singular qualities of the individual are significant. Variations do emerge out of the indistinct night. Each individual is consecrated to a unique task which only he can perform. There is justification for leadership and authority.[3]

Korah misunderstood the Jewish philosophy of power and leadership. He identified power with kingship, and leadership with political authority, Since political power is based upon implied (if not actual) violence involving latent (or actual) physical force, and/or threats of oppression and suppression, Korah claimed that the *k'dushat avot* precluded the right of any one person to such authority. Moses actually agreed with Korah on this point. What Korah failed to realize is that in the "covenantal," or "teaching," community—in contrast to the political community, wherein the warrior or king is the leader—the teacher is the leader. Our tradition tells us that King David was also a *rav* and a *posek*. Members of the covenantal community are not subjects but disciples who voluntarily choose to listen to their master. The rebbe does not raise himself above others. The challenge of "Why do you raise yourself above God's assembly?" is simply inapplicable.

In the case of *g'dolei Yisrael*, the community raises them. This is a spiritual, not political, kingship. Although Moses was a king in a political sense (compare Deuteronomy 33:5) he has always been known as *Moshe Rabbeinu*, Moses our teacher, not *Moshe ha-Melekh*, Moses the King. The political king of the Jews is, at most, a *melekh evyon*, subservient to the real *melekh elyon*. What elevated Moses was his spiritual uniqueness, his teaching role, not his political role. He established a truly genuine *rebbe-talmid* (teacher-disciple) relationship.[4]

Of course a leader must have knowledge and common sense. But it is the Torah role that makes him a leader. Our Torah regards such authority as legitimate. Thus egalitarianism is respected while religious anarchy is avoided.

Korah's Second Argument

The text of the Torah has Korah challenging the right of Moses to rule. A derivative of this argument is that everyone, not only Moses, is entitled to interpret halakha. If holiness is distributed equally to all Jews, and no Jew is raised above another Jew, then the capability of rendering halakhic decisions by using common sense is their's also. Thus the Koraḥ rebellion formulated an ideology with mass appeal. The Midrash relates that Koraḥ assembled his followers and dressed them all in blue (*t'kheilet*) garments which required *tzitziot* (compare Numbers 15:38–41). They all went before Moses and asked him if the *tzitzit* of an all-blue garment still require the prescribed solitary blue thread. Moses' reply in the affirmative was met with ridicule.

A similar question was then posed regarding a house filled with Torah scrolls. Does such a structure require a *m'zuza* on its doorposts? Again Moses' reply was ridiculed by all assembled because his affirmative ruling ran counter to common sense and plain logic.

Koraḥ thus posited that any intelligent person could interpret halakha using common sense; that halakhic analysis was an exoteric competence derived from empirical experience. This is a view echoed by modern day "ritual committees" or the "responsa commissions" of those unlearned in the intricacies of the halakha. They call their approach "creative halakha."

In Hebrew we have three terms denoting mental endowment (compare Ex. 35:31): (1) "*Da'at*" refers to basic intelligence and common sense—a *ben* (or *bar*) *da'at* is a person possessing normal intelligence, "*nitrifa da'ato*" means one who has lost his reason; (2) "*ḥakhma*" suggests specialized knowledge, scholarship; (3) "*bina*" is ascribed to intellect trained in precision, exactness, and distinction. Koraḥ pleaded the case of *da'at*, thereby empowering all to decide on Jewish law.

This appeal to common sense is not only a contemporary phenomenon. It dates back to Sadducean times and even earlier. In one of their disputes with the Sadducees, the Rabbis ruled that since the line of inheritance proceeded through the son, the daughter of the son takes precedence over the deceased's own daughter (that is, a granddaughter would inherit before a daughter). Using a more logical *a fortiori* argument, the Sadducees argued—in vain—that if it is conceivable that a granddaughter, the daughter of the deceased's son can inherit his property, that is, that she can be considered an heir to the deceased because she is his issue's issue, *a fortiori* his own issue (that is, the deceased's daughter) should certainly inherit his property and should take precedence over the granddaughter (*Baba Batra* 115).

Logically the Sadducees were right. Halakha, however, is not always identical with common sense. The halakhic system has its own methodology and manner of analysis, and its own schemata and conceptualized rationale, similar to mathematical constructions. An analogy from the history of science will be helpful in explaining this point.

Aristotelian physics proved faulty because it was governed by common sense. Objects fell, according to this approach, because they had weight;. *Prima facie*, this is an eminently reasonable approach—conclusively disproved by Galileo and Newton. Galileo and Newton replaced a face-value understanding of natural phenomena with abstract scientific laws. They substituted a logos with conceptualization of reality for a commonsense approach. Heat and sound and even matter are but configurations created by the human mind and expressed in mathematical terms which correspond to the external reality. Similarly, the Oral Law has its own epistemological approach, divinely prescribed and conceptually understood, which only a *lamdan* who has mastered its material and methodology can properly grasp. Halakha has its own logos, its own method of thinking. It is more than a mere collection of laws, in the same way that physics is more than an accumulation of laws. Both are autonomous, self-integrated systems. Consequently halakha need not conform to the dictates of commonsense reasoning any more than mathematical or scientific conceptualized systems need accommodate themselves to common sense.[5]

In his *tallit* and *m'zuza* challenges, Korah was arguing on behalf of religious subjectivism, proclaiming the faith, the inner emotional experience, as paramount. "God desires the heart" (*"Rahmana liba ba'i"*; *Sanhedrin* 106b). According to this approach, the mitzva, the outer deed, is secondary to the inner feeling. It has value only insofar as it reflects or stimulates or otherwise relates to one's inner mood. In such a context, the mitzva lacks its own integrity and sanctity, and is no more than a useful tool for eliciting an inner experience. What follows from this reasoning is that the mitzva form should be modified in accordance with changing times and even according to the varying subjectivities of different individuals. Is this not precisely the argument of the deviationists today who are ready to reinterpret, provide substitutions for, or entirely discard mitzvot, presuming some higher moral objective under the guise of *Rahmana liba ba'i*? They use "common sense" to gauge the utility, relevance, and "therapeutic value" of each mitzva. Korah argued that if the goal of *t'kheilet* is to remind us of God, why limit it to one thread? Achieve the objective, evoke the feeling, arouse the emotion, and do so many times over by dyeing the entire garment! Logically Korah was right, if, and this is crucial, the only purpose of the deed is to reflect the experience.

Actually, however, it is the external mitzva, not the inner experience which is primary. The Torah acknowledges a tension between objectivity (that is, the external, physical mitzva prescribed in the *Shulhan Arukh*) and subjectivity (that is, the unique personal *d'veikut* [literally, cleaving, attaching; including the close ultimate relationship with God]). Both interact; there is a romance between finity-the mitzva, and infinity *d'veikut*. In the life of man, they are inseparable.

For example, the obligatory recitation of the Shema is strictly a physical verbal performance, but its fulfillment is internal ("ba-lev," literally, "in the heart"). All of prayer is "service of the heart" ("avoda she-ba-lev"). The laws of mourning (avelut) or of rejoicing or the festivals (simḥat yom tov) are expressed through deeds, though their fulfillment is an emotion. The mitzva is the realized experience, and the emotion itself, a reflection of the mitzva. It is the external act which is primary, while the emotion itself seeks to interpret and reflect the act. The only solid reality is the mitzva, whose integrity and dimensions the halakha can control. The intangible and vacillating inner emotion must follow, reflect, and be disciplined by, the outer mitzva. This is a ḥiddush not commonly understood.

Why doesn't halakha give primacy to the emotion, to the inner feeling? After all, isn't d'veikut a more genuine and authentic experience for the person than his outward acts? There are several answers.

First, the religious emotion even within one individual is volatile, ever changing, and unstable. To correlate the outward act to the inner emotion would require continuous vacillating adjustment, thereby destroying the mitzva's identity. Second, each person experiences things differently. We would continually have to change rituals to reflect the feelings of different people at different times. No monistic communal (k'hilla) service of God would be possible since group worship presupposes a unifying constancy. As Moses said to Koraḥ: "The heathens have many forms of worship and consequently many priests, and cannot therefore assemble to worship together in one temple. We, however, have but one God, one ark, one Law, one altar, and therefore but one High Priest" (Rashi, Numbers 16:6).

Koraḥ's suggestion, however, would fragmentize Jewish worship. The result of each man "doing his own thing,"

though subjectively valid for himself, is that his worship is
unrelated to the worship of his neighbor.

But there is another reason for giving priority to the mitzva-
act. We have no really reliable gauges for differentiating the
intensely felt hedonistic frenzy from the intensely felt religious
experience. There are hypnotic experiences, of the arts, or
under the influence of drugs, which may be confused with
religious experiences. The experience of beauty and the
thrill of beautiful music are at root secular emotions. Pagans
had such orgiastic ceremonials and debauching rituals that
they identified as religious experiences. The essence of idolatry
is this confusing of secular stimulation with actual *d'veikut*
with *Ha-Shem*.

Spengler (in his *Decline of the West*) wrote that Gothic
cathedrals were intended to arouse feelings of infinity and
boundlessness, a sense of questing for the heavens. Similarly,
the goal of organ music, church art, and rhythmic dances
are designed to prepare one for the religious experience.

But such objectives are not attained. The secular experience
remains secular and does not move on to a religious
experience. The Torah wants the religious experience to
emerge out of itself, that is, out of a religious awareness
and not out of aesthetic craving or external stimulants. The
architecture of the synagogue was never important to the
Jew, the modern fashion of building grand edifices
notwithstanding. The piety of the Jew was not a reflection
of his surroundings. The religious experience is autonomous
and independent. It follows upon and reflects the deed, not
the reverse. To pray and then to dance and sing—yes. To
dance and sing in order to pray—no!

The deed is finity, bounded and precisely circumscribed.
D'veikut is infinity, reaching into the beyond. Moses' ruling
was to perform the mitzva of *tzitzit* by wearing a garment
with one thread of blue, for this will lead to *d'veikut* and

infinity. The Jew must move from action to feeling. This achievement is veiled in mystery, but such is the power of a mitzva. But if we substitute common sense for the halakha, then even an entire garment of *t'kheilet* will not do. Seeing a single thread of blue within the context of a proper performance of the mitzva produces a great experience. Blue without the mitzva can produce bizarre, even vulgar, reactions and modes of expression. We may be affected then in many ways, but *d'veikut* cannot be achieved. Koraḥ lacked the patience to master the unique halakhic conceptual system. He was not a *lamdan.* Koraḥ wanted to do to halakha what Aristotle did to physics. So too, all the pseudo-halakhists of our own day who prescribe all forms of "amendments" to the halakhic system.

The Incense and the Candelabra

In Exodus (30:7) we read: ". . . every morning when Moses fixes the candelabra he shall cause the incense to ascend." These were the two duties of the High Priest. Kindling the *menora* (the candelabra) symbolizes light, knowledge, clarity of concept, and depth of analysis. In short, it symbolizes the halakhic mitzva performance. The incense reflects the mysterium in creation, the human being reaching out for *d'veikut* with God Who is the source of all existence. It symbolizes the colorful, subjective, religious emotion.

The Torah thus says coordinate the two, the incense with the candelabra, the subjective with the objective, the experience with the deed, the passion with the performance, the romance with the outer discipline. First (in the mitzva of *tzitzit*) comes "and you shall look upon them," a deed performance, and then, only then, will the recollection of the mitzvot, the experience, come.

NOTES

1. See Numbers 10:29, where Moses pleads with Yitro to accompany them into the Promised Land. The texts suggests that this move was to be imminently realized.

2. See, for example, Leviticus 19:20 and 27:33.

3. In the conversion process (*gerut*) both aspects of *k'dusha*, the social and the individual, are acquired. Circumcision, a sign of identity with the group, attaches one to the group. A share of *k'dusha* may be drawn from the community, and the Patriarchs become the convert's forefathers. Immersion, however, symbolizes a momentary withdrawal from the community for a direct, individual, confrontation with God for the receiving of the individual *k'dusha*.

4. See, for example, Deuteronomy 17:9 and Malachi 2:7.

5. The argument advanced by Women's Liberation members that the halakhic ineligibility of women to serve as witnesses (*pasul eidut*) indicates feminine inferiority is based upon common sense and is of course wrong. Since male and female alike were created in God's image (Genesis 1:27)—the only basis of ultimate worth—both have equal infinite endowments. The fact that even an anointed king (*melekh mashuah*)—including Moses, King David, and King Solomon—is ineligible to be a witness suggests that the reasons for disqualification are not related to one's relative worthiness. The woman's exclusion from the public, political realm emerges out of the unique halakhic structure which has an esoteric justification not subject to commonsense evaluation.

Similarly, the ineligibility of women to be counted in a *minyan* excludes Hana who was our foremost teacher of the art and manner of prayer! This is not rational or commonsensical. Rather it is a derivation from a unique conceptualized structure which operates on its own imperatives.

Aseret ha-Dibrot

What follows is a journalistic editing of privately circulated notes of the Rav's 1970 Saturday night Boston lectures of June 6, 13, 20. The text is the 20th chapter of *Exodus*

Verse 1: "And *Elokim* spoke all these words, saying." Rashi comments, "The word '*Elokim*' is a term for a judge. There are chapters in the Torah of such a nature that if a person observes the commandment contained there, he will receive a reward, but if he does not observe them, he will not be punished: one might therefore think that the *Aseret ha-Dibrot* are also of such a character, hence Scripture states '*Elokim* spoke': God, who is a judge exacting punishment."

The problem with which Rashi and the *Mekhilta* (from which he quotes) are dealing is the fact that throughout the portion of *Yitro*, especially in the section dealing with the giving of the Torah, the term "*Ha-Shem*" is used exclusively, and then, suddenly, we find the term "*Elokim*." *Hazal* were always sensitive to such shifts, as in *B'reshit*, where in the first chapter "*Elokim*" is used and in the second chapter the name "*Ha-Shem Elokim*" is used.

Rashi has pointed out that "*Elokim*" concerns God's relationship with the universe as well as with man, insofar as man forms a part of the universe. Thus "*Elokim*" is the appropriate term for the more general creation story in the first chapter of *B'reshit*. But when one comes to the story of man, his destiny, his experience, then the term "*Ha-Shem*" is used, as this denotes God's relation to man. The term "*Ha-Shem Elokim*" is used in the second chapter of *B'reshit*, as it indicates a complete universe, one which contains animate and inanimate nature on the one hand, and man on the other. Thus the use of "*Ha-Shem*" in connection with the giving of the Torah shows that this event was not part of God's relation with nature, but rather a consequence of His relation with man. But then the use of "*Elokim*" for the *Aseret ha-Dibrot* is troublesome.

Rambam refers to *mitzvat r'shut*, a paradoxical term meaning "a commandment whose fulfillment is voluntary." An example of this would be *shiluah ha-kan*. If one wants eggs from a nest, he must first send the mother away; but if he does not want the eggs, there is nothing to be done. Similarly, the mitzva of sukka (except for the first night.) If one wants to eat bread then he must sit in a sukka and recite a special blessing. But if one is willing to forgo bread and cereals, there is no punishment for not having a sukka. The Torah allows one to "avoid" these mitzvot.

Mizrahi and other commentators on Rashi assume that Rashi is saying that God feared that the Jews would mistakenly think that *Aseret ha-dibrot* were mitzvot of this nature; hence the shift to "*Elokim*." But most of the *dibrot* are negative commandments; it does not make sense to think that these could be avoided. As for the positive ones, could we really say that if one honors his parents or observes the Shabbat he is rewarded, but if not, he is not punished? Evidently, this interpretation of Rashi is in error.

Rather, Rashi seems to be saying something else. There are some mitzvot for which one is rewarded in this world, but for which disobedience is punished on the day of judgment, in *Olam ha-Ba*. But this is not true of the *Aseret ha-Dibrot*. Those who violate them will be punished in this world as well as in the world to come.

The term "*Elokim*" designates might, force, strength, power, vigor. It designates the natural law, and it is for this reason that this term is used in the first story of creation. But in the Torah, the same term also designates a judge; thus God is the source of justice. He is both natural and moral lawgiver.

Consider natural law. If a man decides to defy the law of gravity and walks over a ledge, the law promptly exacts its claim on him and he falls down. We might call this "natural punishment." The punishment is built into the act; there is no need for extraneous punishment. If a person takes drugs, then even if he does *t'shuva*, the organic and biochemical damage done to the body remains. *Elokim* does not forgive.

Now, if this is true of natural law, it is also true of certain elements of moral law. A murder avenges itself on the murderer. If a man neglects to honor his parents, our Sages say that his children, seeing the way he treats his parents, will not honor him. A person may turn to *avoda zara*, but it will eventually be a means of his own self-destruction. If one does not observe Shabbat, he stays in *ḥol* without a break. At no point does he come into the higher redeemed existence of Shabbat as contrasted to *ḥol*. Rashi's claim, therefore, is that the basic moral law is contained in the *Aseret ha-Dibrot*. The same God is the Author of both the natural and the moral laws. Hence promiscuity, theft, murder, perjury, idol worship, atheism, agnosticism, and so forth must all lead to disaster. At both the cosmic and moral level, it is impossible for any man to fight with God.

"All these words." Rashi says that "this tells us that the Holy One, Blessed Be He, said all these words in one utterance, something a human being cannot do." A human cannot say two things at one time; on the contrary, human speech implies a process, a sequence, a ranked order. Rashi and the *Mekhilta* are saying that there are not ten *dibrot* but one; they cannot be separated, or ordered according to their importance. There are those who say that moral law is good, but not ritual law. But we say that the ethical law and ritual law alike depend on faith in the Almighty. One cannot divorce a commitment to "ethics" from a commitment to "ritual" mitzvot.

"*Lemor*" ("saying"). Rashi says, "This teaches that they answered the positive mitzvot 'Yes' and the negative mitzvot 'No.'" The Jews were expected to respond and to accept each commandment. But the *Mekhilta*, from which Rashi quotes, notes an argument between R. Ishmael and R. Akiva as to what the response of the Jews actually was. R. Ishmael takes the view outlined in Rashi. R. Akiva agrees that they answered "Yes" to the positive mitzvot, but says that they answered "Yes" to the negative mitzvot also. What is the difference between them?

Let us suppose for example, that a father tells his child, "Don't play with Johnny because he is a bad boy." If the child responds, "Oh, no!" he is expressing an innate revulsion: I would not have played with him even it you did not tell me not to. But a response of "Yes" means: Well, since you say so, I will obey you. R. Akiva is saying that since you said "Do not murder," we don't murder; but if you did not say it, we might do it. R. Ishmael says that even without God, man would know better. For R. Akiva, a man is capable of murder and is stopped only because of God.

Today, not much proof is needed of R. Akiva's point of view. There is some devil in man; some satan who can suddenly come to the fore. To prevent this, we need the word of God. For R. Akiva, the *mishpatim*, those rules for which we think we know the reason should be done on the same basis as the *ḥukim*, for which we do not know the reason.

Verse 2: "*Anokhi* am the Lord, your God, who took you out of the Land of Egypt." Rashi says, "This bringing out is alone of sufficient importance that you should subject yourself to Me." Rashi seems to be troubled by God's description of Himself. Why didn't He describe Himself as "Maker of Heaven and Earth"? Ibn Ezra, quoting Yehudah Halevi, says that the reason for this was that the Jews had not experienced

Creation but had experienced the Exodus. Rashi's reasoning is that something special happened to the Jews, so they alone have special mitzvot. Only the Jews left Egypt; only they have the 613 mitzvot.

"Another explanation," continues Rashi, "He had revealed Himself at the Red Sea as a mighty man of war and here He revealed Himself as an elder filled with compassion . . . Do not say 'there are two divine beings.' It is I Who brought you forth from Egypt and Who appeared to you at the Red Sea." Rashi is concerned with why the word *"Anokhi"* is used instead of *"Ani."* In Hebrew, *"ani"* is used when "I" is the subject, but the emphasis is on the action. But *"Anokhi"* is used when one is proclaiming an identity. Here, then, God is proclaiming that He is the same God.

Judaism, as a moral discipline, is not a homogeneous discipline of love and compassion. Judaism is also very practical; it knows that man cannot protect himself with love alone. Today, for example, Jews having no real alternatives are forced to kill Arabs, some of whom may be innocent, or see the entire *Yishuv* eliminated. Our post-Hitlerian age leaves us no choice. Treblinka and Buchenwald have taught the world that if you dislike Jews, don't bother hating or persecuting them—just kill them. The Torah is practical. God appears in two different guises, in two mutually exclusive roles. At Sinai, He revealed Himself as an old teacher full of love and understanding. At the Red Sea He appeared as a mighty warrior. The same God who forbade working an ox on Shabbat killed the Egyptians' horses. But was there an alternative at the Red Sea? The only alternative was to surrender and be killed. Hence the Torah teaches that in such cases you kill the enemy beforehand. The object of war is to win, not to lose. God reconciles the contradiction in Himself for He is the same.

In commenting on verse 20, Rashi notes that "The people

heard the voices—voices coming from the four cardinal
points and from the heavens and the earth. But do not say
there are many deities." The introductory words *"Anokhi
Ha-Shem"* are the root of human morality. At least once in
his life a man hears these words. A man wants to believe in
God as he wants food or freedom. But this intrinsic need
may be precipitated by many factors. One man may respond
to beauty, others to scientific order. Some people find God
in their loneliness; others in their hour of triumph. The
voices come from various directions. God may be found in
science, aesthetics, and morale, in crisis or in triumph. But
he is the same God.

God's glory fills the whole earth; the voices come from all
six directions. But God also "contracts" himself—this is
tzimtzum—and comes to the top of a mountain, a very
small place. This *tzimtzum* exhibits an ethical norm: Just as
God presents himself in both modes, so man must emulate
him in both expansion and in self-limitation. Man is duty
bound to negate himself and not try to manage his own
moral law as modern man is inclined to do.

"Elokekha—your (singular) God." The *Aseret ha-Dibrot* are
repeated not only in *Deuteronomy*, but also in *K'doshim*.
There, however, we find the word *"Elokeikhem,"* (Leviticus
19:4), with "your" in the plural. This should not be surprising,
as both forms of the word are necessary. Suppose God
spoke just to the community. Then the obligation of the
individual would be derived from the community, and one
could argue that if the community as a whole disregards a
mitzva, an individual might feel himself to be exempt. Thus
the need for a simpler form. But the plural form is also
necessary, for it teaches us that we each are responsible for
all Israel. This finds expression in the halakha of *areivut.*
The plural form binds us all to one another.

"Out of a House of Slaves." "They were not slaves to

slaves," says Rashi, "but slaves to the king." What is the distinction? One can be a slave to an individual or to a corporate body such as the state. If one is owned by an individual, he may be exposed to ill-treatment or, on the contrary, be fortunate enough to have a good man as his owner. But a slave to a state, to a cruel, soulless being, has an automatically bad lot. It was out of the condition of being slaves to a soulless being that God took us.

Verse 3: "You shall have no other gods." We must not think that *avoda zara* is limited to idol worship. Whenever anything that is not God is given an absolute value, we have *avoda zara*. "Another explanation of 'other gods,'" says Rashi. "is they are strange to those who worship them; these cry to them, but they do not answer them." This is the "natural punishment" for violating this mitzva: if Jews worship *avoda zara*, it will betray them. One modern example of this is Communism. Many Jews worshipped Communism. But Russia later betrayed them and all Jews.

"*Al Panai*" ("before my face"). Onkelos translates this as "*bar mene*" ("to replace Me," "before Me"). Interestingly, there are many injunctions against idol worship, but none against atheism. When man revolts against God, he may think himself to be free; but soon, even he will build his own idol. It is not atheism that can replace God, but a new godless religion such as Communism.

Rashi's comment is "as long as I exist," forever and ever. "You should not say that only the generation that left Egypt received the commandment against idolatry." The generation reared in freedom might have felt that since they were not raised in an atmosphere of *avoda zara*, this commandment did not apply to them. But the rabbis astutely compared the sex urge to the urge to worship idols; both are constant. Man is tempted to idol worship regardless of his progress and civilization. Indeed, the central impulse to *avoda zara* is rooted in man's need to have faith in someone or something. There are, to be sure, many idols; there are the corporate state, science, utopian society. But the knee must bend; the person who is always upright is the unhappiest person possible. And so this mitzva is directed not only to those who left Egypt, but to all generations. It is directed against the modern man who is a follower of *avoda zara* as well.

Ramban translates this phrase as "in my presence." But God is ubiquitous, so how could this or anything be done not in His presence? The rabbis equated *avoda zara* with adultery. There are two aspects of adultery. The first involves breach of contract, the violation and desecration of a commitment. The other aspect is the humiliation of the cheated partner. The first is a fact whether or not the cheated partner knows of it. But to be humiliated, one must know about it. The whole earth is full of His glory. Idol worship is performed in God's presence, no matter where the physical activities take place, and so it is especially humiliating and offensive to Him.

The second point in Ramban's comment is that at every level, in every walk of life, God confronts man. At every stage of life, He interferes and tells man how to live, how to conduct his family life, his relations with his workers, and so on. There is no freedom from God's command.

Verse 7: "You shall not take the name of the Lord your God in vain; for God will not consider him guiltless who takes His name in vain." Onkelos translates the first "in vain" as "*l'magana*" ("in vain") and the second as "*l'shikra*" ("falsely"). Rashi says "for no reason, idly." There are really two different offenses: *sheker* and *shav*. *Sheker* involves deceit. It is a statement which is not true, but which could be true. *Shav*, on the other hand, involves an obvious lie, such as swearing that a black book is red. It exposes one to humiliation and ridicule and degrades and corrupts the human personality. A man does not own himself; he belongs to God, and consequently, actions such as this involving self-degradation are forbidden.

But there is another aspect of *shav*, this is to swear to an obvious truth. A man should not talk in stereotypes and cliches. A teacher should not teach if he could not add anything to human knowledge. If you have nothing to say, do not repeat what everyone knows. It is a violation of human dignity. Modern man is increasingly losing his individuality; he repeats what the news media tell him. The Torah wants one to preserve his individuality. A person should be sure that what he says is meaningful.

Verse 8: "Remember the Shabbat day to keep it holy." Rashi comments: "'Remember' and 'Observe' were spoken in one utterance." "*Zakhor*," which implies preparing in advance, is inseparable from "*Shamor*," which refers to the technical observance of Shabbat, refraining from work and other, similar matters. Without "*Shamor*" there is no possibility of a real Shabbat experience.

God does not need our surrender; it is we who need it. God gives man the world for six days. On the seventh, man returns the world to God. *K'dusha* is literally an act of withdrawal. On Shabbat, man withdraws, but in a positive way--to *k'dusha*, Torah, prayer.

There is a passage in the Shabbat *Minha* prayer. "You are One, and Your name is One, and who is like Your people Israel, one on earth." Shabbat takes us out of the normal world and reminds us of our unique destiny.

The Covenantal Community

On November 12, 1973, the Rav delivered the following lecture to the Rabbinic Alumni of Yeshiva University. The theme of the presentation was "Insights into the *Sedra* of *Hayei Sara.*"

We are all members of a covenant that God established with Abraham. We see that there are two covenants; the first, which God concluded with the Patriarchs, and the second, which God concluded with Moses on Mt. Sinai. The nature of the Sinaitic covenant was a commitment to the fulfillment of commandments. It is a bond of obligation. The patriarchal covenant, on the other hand, has no commandments included in it, with the exception of circumcision. Yet the two are connected. At the Sinitic covenant, it says *"v'zakharti et b'riti"* ("I will remember my former covenants"). It specifically mentions there the Patriarchal covenant. The Sinitic covenant relates to the human deed. The patriarchal covenant relates to the fundamental essence of a person. It teaches man how to feel, or to experience, as a human being. The Sinitic covenant teaches us how to act in the Jewish community. The Patriarchal covenant teaches us how to feel our Jewishness.

Man and woman are both included in the covenant, just as they are together included in the Creation. Adam alone would never have been accorded the title of Man. Human experience is a dual one. The fact that "in the image of God" applied to both male and female shows that Judaism never considered woman the inferior sex. They were both created not because they differ physically, but rather metaphysically. They represent a dual destiny which together form one perfect ideal. The covenant cannot be carried on by Ishmael, who represents only Abraham. It requires Isaac, who represents both Abraham and Sara. No covenant is possible without her. Also, we are told about the change in Sara's name in the past tense, for it had already taken place at the same time that Abraham's name had been changed. Not only did man and woman achieve dignity together at creation, but also the covenant of God was formed with both.

When Sara died, Abraham not only lost his wife but also realized that he had completed his covenantal role. Abraham outlived Sara by 38 years, yet no events are recorded about his life in this period, with the exception of the purchase of a burial ground for Sara—the *M'arat ha-Makhpela*—and the acquisition of Rivka for Isaac. The latter was important not for Abraham's sake, but rather because of Rivka. The Patriarchal covenant could now continue and be passed on to Isaac and Rivka. No other events related to Abraham are recorded, because his task had been completed. Upon the death of Sara, the Torah says, "And Abraham came to mourn for Sara and to weep for her" ("*lispod l'Sara v'livkota*"). *B'khiya* is not mourning. It is an emotional outburst of feeling, a relief of tension. *Hesped*, on the other hand, is calculated thought of what has been lost. Abraham mourned his personal loss, but he was also concerned about the covenant with God. Without Sara no covenant is possible. What Abraham did first was *lispod*. First he appraised the situation, as to her contribution to society, mourning in objective terms. In this, all could share with him. Then—only after he had made a reevaluation—did he first mourn his own tremendous personal loss.

What role did God assign to Sara? What kind of a person was she? The first comment by Rashi in this weekly portion says, "At 100 she was like 20 with regard to sin . . . and at 20 she was like 7 with regard to beauty." This whole midrash is very strange. First of all, might we not suggest a better *girsa*, stating that at 100 she was like 20 with regard to beauty, and at 20 she was like 7 with regard to sin. But still even with the old text, what does the midrash want to convey to us? Normally when we say *"sh'nei ḥayei Sara"* ("the years of the life of Sara"), it would answer for us the question of how old Sara was. But in this case this would be redundant because we had just been told the answer to this question. Here, the question is "Who was Sara? What were her characteristics?" The answer is she was a very strange girl. She was a seven-year-old innocent child even when she was twenty. And even when she was ripe in years, she was still a twenty-year-old lady. The biography of Sara is told in three short words-*sh'nei ḥayei Sara*. Maturity did not destroy the child. She grew up, developed, and matured. As an adult she might have reached the greatest intellectual heights, but this development did not destroy her experiences of childhood. She retained within her personality the young bold outlook of a youthful girl of twenty. For her—the covenantal woman—these experiences of the different ages were not one followed by the other. Rather, they existed simultaneously within her. And this is the description of the covenantal character.

We have here four basic types of commandments—learning, prayer, faith, and love. Learning, *talmud Torah*, is an intellectual process. For learning you need a mature mind. The ideal is a man ripe in years who has already accumulated a wealth of knowledge. The trained mind of an adult is what is desired. In *talmud Torah* we must not be so obedient. We must have the ability to criticize. We see how Rav Yoḥanan sorely missed his companion Resh Lakish, who constantly argued with him. Reb Elazar ben Pedat, who always agreed with him, was of no consolation to him. Torah was given to man because he can achieve great heights.

However, when it comes to prayer, we find another situation. We have forgotten the art of prayer When one prays, the scenery changes completely. The adult, proud mind, the genius, is not admitted to the sanctuary of prayer. Prayer requires self-negation, helplessness. It is generated by despairing. Prayer is surrendering. It is the realization that one is finite and valueless that is the spring-well of prayer. The only one who knows how to pray is the infant. The infant realizes that his existence is dependent on someone else.

There is also another act which only a child is capable of. This is *emuna*. Faith is complete reliance and trust in someone. We can only have faith in God. A little infant, for example, can have absolute faith in his mother. And this is what is required for prayer But faith requires more than this. It requires suspension of judgment and suspension of logic. You must act even though you may not understand. You must at times do away with the principle of passing judgment. Only man-child has this ability. The adult, in relation to God, must act in this manner. Such a performance was required of Abraham. Abraham no doubt preached against murder and the pagan practice of child sacrifice. Furthermore, God had told Abraham that through Isaac he would become the father of a great people. So how could he now be expected to go and offer this same Isaac on an altar as a sacrifice? Yet Abraham did not ask for any explanation. Indeed, he did not utter a single word. He suspended his logic, his own humanity, and was willing to sacrifice Isaac. Only a child could have this total faith. Today, too, we should not try to rationalize all commandments. This lack of willingness to suspend judgment has been the seed to the radical changes being proposed by the Conservative movement. Abraham, who had mature ripe judgment, was able to transform himself to a child when necessary.

Torah requires manhood and maturity, childhood and innocence Sara was at 100 like at 20. At the same time full of vigor and yet mature and resolved. The little child cannot fight for justice. Neither can the old man. Only the young man, the twenty year old, could merge all these qualities. When Abraham fought in battle, he fought like a youngster.

What kind of a person is the covenantal man and woman? He has an awareness of greatness and at the same time an awareness of helplessness. And this is the biography of Sara Throughout her whole life, she was seven, she was twenty, and she was one hundred. We, too, must merge these qualities together and form the perfect being.

There is a great difference between historical dynamics and covenantal destiny. In historical dynamics one event follows another. History is viewed as mechanical. The past is responsible for the present. However, the covenantal event is sustained by the covenantal promise. The future is responsible for the present. For example, the experience of the Land of Israel is a covenantal one. It cannot be explained in terms of historical dynamics. The cause of Eretz Yisrael is not an event of the land but rather its cause is the fulfillment of a promise. The covenant has created a new concept—destiny, meaning destination. What determines the historical experience of the Jew is not the point of departure but rather the destination of k'lal Yisrael.

Jews have always lived among Gentiles and dealt with them, just as Abraham deal with Efron. Consequently, we share in the historical experiences such as famine, war, and immorality with the rest of mankind. We have no right to tell mankind that these problems are delegated for non-Jews only. The trouble with our non-Jewish neighbors is that they can't understand the holiness of our covenantal commitment. They view us as a strange, enigmatic people, and would like us to identify with them.

Yet Abraham realized that you can have the covenantal commitment in addition to the universal one. When he said to his lads, "Sit ye here with the donkey and I and the boy will go yonder," the two lads only had a general commitment of "here," representing the present, the universal commitment, whereas Abraham and Isaac were also reaching for "yonder" representing the future, the covenantal commitment, as well.

The Unique Experience of Judaism

In a unique lecture given on April 26, 1972, Rabbi Soloveitchik described the experiential, cognitive and functional frameworks found in Judaism. This lecture was given to members of the Yolanda Benson Honor Society, a group of high school and college age youth who have become *ba'alei t'shuva* through the Torah Leadership Seminar Program sponsored by the Youth Bureau of Yeshiva University.

Time Awareness

Judaism apprehended youth and old age not only as successive physiological periods in a person's life; Judaism understood them in spiritual terms as well. As such, they describe two existential moods, two "I awarenesses": the one of a youth, the other of an old man. Organically, youth and old age are, of course, mutually exclusive. Youth is primarily the time of tissue buildup, and old age, the time of tissue destruction. However, as existential moods they can be experienced simultaneously, and as "I awarenesses" they may exist contemporaneously in the same individual.

These different existential awarenesses are determined by different time awarenesses. While grammar uses three tenses (past, present, future), existentially, the present lies in the past or in the future and cannot be isolated as a separate experience. What we call the present is only a vantage point from which we look forward or backward. Time is experienced by us in retrospection as a memory or recollection, and in expectation and anticipation as a vision of events which will transpire some time hence.

The time awareness of youth is future oriented while the time awareness of the old centers on the past. Existentially, to be young means to be committed to the future, while to be old means to contemplate what once was but is no longer. The young man is essentially a searcher, a questioner, and a believer, while the old man is primarily a reviewer, a meditator, and a skeptic.[1]

Judaism attempts to combine the experience of youth and age and requires of the Jew that he be simultaneously, and perhaps paradoxically, both young and old. Like a tree whose roots absorb their nourishment from the soil and whose foliage is caressed by sunlight flowing from a distant and unknown future, the Jew must be deeply rooted in his past and inspired by a vision of the future.

The time awareness of Judaism is *recollection* and *anticipation*, and it may be best understood by positing (and analyzing) two doctrines: the doctrine of *experiential memory* and the doctrine of *experiential anticipation*.

Experiential Memory

In order to understand what experiential memory is, we must recognize that there are two kinds of memory. The first is an intellectual memory which mechanically recalls and assembles factual data. The other memory recalls experiences by evoking the feelings of the past event. Judaism insisted that Jews recall not only the factual events of the past, but that in addition the experiences of the past retain their vigor undiminished despite the passage of time. Whatever was horrible and frightening should be remembered as horrible and frightening, no matter how much time has elapsed since the event transpired. The memory of what once was therapeutic and redemptive should forever possess those qualities. In short, when remembering the past, the Jew relives the event as if it were a present reality.

Many halakhot are clearly related to experiential memory.[2] Our commitment to *Eretz Yisrael*—one of the strangest phenomena in human psychology—is intelligible only in

terms of experiential memory. We have been exiled from
the land of Israel for 1900 years and suddenly we discovered
that it is our home. What is responsible is not the memory
of events which occurred there or people who lived there
3,000 years ago. For the non-Jew, these are merely
archeological facts. For the Jew, they are experiential facts.
Biblical stories are in our present. In the *ḥeder* we cried
when we learned of the sale of Joseph, and we rejoiced in
his ascendancy to power. There was a freshness, a vigor, a
nearness which we felt in that drama. The ninth of Av was
not a story out of antiquity; we witnessed the tragedy. In
our childish eyes we saw the flames enveloping the Holy of
Holies. There was participation and involvement as if we
had been transferred back in time to the year 70 C.E.

As a matter of fact this is the only way to study the Bible.
Intellectual analysis, while indispensable, will not suffice to
uncover the spiritual kerygma of the Bible. Only one who
can read between the lines, who can experience the biblical
event and can establish communion with its characters can
discover and fully comprehend the biblical message.

Experiential Anticipation

Just as the past can be experienced in the present, so can
the future. Experiential anticipation means that the Jew
anticipates an event not just because it is bound to occur—that
would only be an intellectual anticipation; it means that the
Jew becomes excited and rejoices and sings and dances as
if an event which will first transpire on some unknown date
in the future had already actually taken place. The future is
experienced as reality and is integrated into the frame of
reference of reality even before it occurs. The mother who
learns of her child's unexpected homecoming experiences
the joy of his "resurrection" even before he opens the door.

Experiential memory commits the Jew to reliving his past,

and experiential anticipation, the requirement of preexperience, commits the Jew to the future.

This identification of the Jew with the past and his commitment to the future is a challenge, not a gratuity, and it therefore requires dedication and sacrifice. Although basically an emotional experience, time awareness must be merged with knowledge and cognition. A Jew must study in order to achieve the aforementioned synthesis and reconciliation. Notwithstanding the importance Judaism attached to the emotions, their fleeting and transient nature led Judaism to distrust them. While Pascal spoke of a logic *du coeur*, a logic of the heart, Judaism requires a logic and ethics of the heart. All feelings—joy, sadness, anger, compassion—must be enlightened, and all need to be controlled by man. Subjectivism which is not guided by logic may become destructive, even in the search for Torah. The cognitive gesture must be involved in our time experience. This can be achieved only through study, especially of *Humash*. Ancient events must be understood in modern categories, and current events must be interpreted via biblical categories. It is most important to be able to see in the *Humash* the mirror of human destiny in general, and of Jewish destiny in particular. A sensitivity to seeing life reflected in the *Humash* must be developed.

With one hand the Jew receives the message of the past, and with the other he passes it on to the future. Through the merging of experiential memory and experiential anticipation the Jew transcends temporal bounds and penetrates into eternity.

Halakha

Judaism is not only an experiential adventure; it is a cognitive, intellectual adventure as well. In a certain sense, Judaism is almost identical with thought. No other religious denomination understands "*lomdus*" or has anything comparable to it, and unless one is already familiar with it it seems so strange a discipline that it defies complete explanation.

One could point to the Talmud in answering the question "What is halakha?" but this would be as insufficient as answering the question "What is physics?" by taking the questioner to the library and pointing to the shelves containing Newton's *Principia*, Einstein's theory of relativity, Planck's quantum mechanics, and Maxwell's equations and saying, "This is physics!" Even a definition of Physics as "the system of rules and laws pertaining to the functioning of nature," while not incorrect, is not correct either. Such a definition describes an aspect of Physics, but not all of it.

An understanding of what mathematics is will help. Mathematics is not a list of equations; it is a method of thinking. The same is true of physics. Physics is a peculiar way of interpreting natural phenomena by quantifying the qualitative contents of nature, thereby converting the latter into categories which fit the temporal-spatial relational system of physics.

Halakha too is best understood as a mode of thinking, a way of interpreting man and his environment.[3] Halakha has its own unique approach to the study of man and the world, and its own method of forming value judgments and determining moral worth. The halakhic methodological approach demands the highest levels of abstraction and conceptualization. Halakhic logic is a peculiar method of analysis which is very difficult and very abstract. While halakha frames laws which are clearly meant to be acted out, it is at root a Divine method of thought.

The role of the *talmid ḥakham* proves the importance of halakha (as a system of thought) in Judaism. The covenantal community is a teaching community. The role of the political community is to protect the teaching community. Thus the central figure in the covenantal community is the teacher or prophet, not the warlord or king. Indeed Judaism revolves around the *rebbe-talmid*, teacher-disciple relationship, and the foremost example of this was the relationship established between Moses and the Children of Israel.

Mitzvot

Thus far we have seen that Judaism is unique both as an experiential as well as a scholastic community. We shall now see that Judaism is also unique as an acting community also.

It is not enough to experience time in a peculiar fashion, or to perfect a unique method of analysis. The Jew must practice, and again he is unique. The uniqueness of his practice is expressed in three ways.

1. There is no distinction between the sacral and the secular. That dichotomy is a Christian concept, invented by the founder of Christianity when he claimed that one should render unto Caesar his due and unto God, His. Unfortunately, the result of such a split is that people usually end up following Caesar and not God. Indeed this division between the ecclesiastical and political, the religious and the secular, is directly responsible for the failure of Christianity. The necessary result of man projecting a double image, one vis-à-vis Caesar and another vis-à-vis God, is that man develops a schism within himself, his actions become contradictory, and he becomes entangled in a web of hypocrisy. He comes to believe in Caesar and God equally.

What is sacred or profane in Judaism depends upon man's actions. If man so desires, God will abide in his office, on the assembly line, or in the halls of Congress. No boundaries will keep God out if man wants His presence. But if man does not want His presence, God will absent Himself even from the synagogue, even from the Holy of Holies. Judaism embraces the totality of life, not just areas of ritual concern. Two full volumes of *Hoshen Mishpat* deal with labor and business ethics, legal procedure, and laws of testimony. Judaism cannot be squeezed into the synagogue. The synagogue is just an institution and Judaism's claim upon the totality of human life includes the office, the factory, the kitchen, and the bedroom.

2. Detail is important in Judaism. The model for the religious ritual in Judaism is the mathematical model, the characteristic of which is precision. No one would dare to cross a bridge which was not built with precision. In Judaism religious ceremony depends upon the detail. In contrast to the mathematical model is the esthetic model. In esthetics the overall configuration, the gestalt, is important, not the detail. Indeed, one steps back to view a painting so that the detail disappears. If the detail is too compelling it disrupts the overall effect. Halakhically, the detail is important. One minute before sunset Friday eve and one minute after is the difference between identical acts being permitted or forbidden. The difference between the Conservative approach and ours may be understood in light of the above. They have attempted to refashion Judaism into the esthetic experience. For them, the whole is important, not the detail. An hour after sunset all may be permitted as long as the table is set and candles are lit. Theirs is an artistic, esthetic approach, not a halakhic one.

It is not that we lack appreciation of the esthetic experience. We do enjoy the beautiful, but much beauty is false and Judaism demands truth. The halakhic model is like the ethical and mathematical models, where precision and concern with detail are all-important. The ethical violation is identical whether ten thousand dollars or a few pennies were stolen. Just as truth demands precision and is concerned with trivia, so too halakhic thinking is rigorous and halakhic action is expressed via the detail.

3. Unlike general religious practice, Jewish observance consists mainly of inaction rather than action, of withdrawal rather than surging forward. Although Judaism consists of positive and negative precepts, the latter are the more important. The first law given to Adam was a prohibition.[4] The negative precepts are at the core of Judaism, because they require a greater effort and demand a more sacrificial spirit than the positive commandments. William James saw happiness as the goal of religion. Judaism sees greatness as the goal. Not the greatness of business or political or military success but the greatness of heroism of the spirit. The acid test for moral heroism or cowardice is compliance with the negative precepts, since they compel man to engage in heroic restraint. This is especially true in the realm of sexual morality where enormous self control is necessary to control the almost overpowering sexual drive, and where the halakha is almost ruthlessly strict. Judaism is not concerned with what is not heroic.

Having said this much, we must recognize that there are two kinds of heroism. One kind is the spectacular and glorious heroism of which minstrels sing on street corners and troubadours recite in the marketplace. This heroism consists of bold, dramatic actions, of publicly defying evil and unjustness, of being ready to suffer and accept martyrdom as a consequence.

The other kind of heroism is nonspectacular, and has produced historically meager results. The decisions are insignificant except for the party involved. This heroism consists primarily of giving up something very precious at the moment of achieving the highest joy. It occurs unnoticed by others in private chambers and in a solitude of mind.

Judaism recognizes both kinds of heroism. The prophets and the ten martyrs (*asara harugei malkhut*) displayed the first kind of heroism, and we are all aware of their heroism. The second kind of heroism is known only to God. Only He is aware of it, and only He can appreciate it.

The midrash (*P'tihuta d'Eikha Rabati*) relates that after the *Bet ha-Mikdash* was destroyed and the Jews were exiled, each of the Patriarchs came before God to plead with him. Each enumerated his achievements and recounted his sacrifices. God ignored their pleas. But to Rachel's appeal, God responded.

Why was her prayer immediately accepted? What could she tell that could make her story more exalted than those told by the architects of our nation? What was so exceptional in her biography? The answer, says the midrash, is that Rachel recalled how, in order to spare her sister embarrassment and humiliation, she disclosed to Leah the password that would identify her to Jacob. By what virtue did this story transcend the stories told by the Patriarchs and Moses? The answer lies in the Torah's appreciation of nonspectacular heroism. The heart of young Rachel was saturated with love for Jacob, yet she gave that up so as not to humiliate her sister. No one watches the young couple on a date. It is simple to violate the law, especially if one is driven by an urge which is basically animalistic. Self-control at such a moment is very much appreciated by God.

NOTES

1. The two books of the Bible that reflect these moods are the Song of Songs and Ecclesiastes. Solomon wrote the former in his youth, and the latter when he was an old man.

2. [Two examples often cited by the Rav have been the mourning laws we observe on Tisha B'Av—the concrete halakhic actions reflecting an inner anguish—and the halakhic requirement upon every Jew to reexperience the Exodus from Egypt at the Passover Seder.]

3. [An extended development of the parallel between the halakhic and the physical-mathematical modes of thinking is to be found in *Ma Dodech Midod* and especially in *Ish HaHalakha*. The independent a priori nature of the halakhic system and its method of quantifying otherwise "qualitative" concepts are fully discussed there. See also "The First Rebellion against Torah Authority" in this volume.]

4. On another occasion the Rav developed a related idea along the following lines:

Judaism places little significance in the ceremonial, emphasizing discipline instead. A good example is of course the observance and nonviolation of Shabbat. Another example is *g'zeirah d'Rabah*. [Rabah banned the blowing of the shofar on Rosh Hashana and the taking of the lulav on Sukkot when these holidays coincided with Shabbat. He feared that some individuals, unlearned in the proper performance of the mitzva, might carry the ceremonial mitzva object through a public thoroughfare—a breach of the Shabbat *m'lakha*-discipline—to a house of one knowledgeable in the laws of the mitzva, for instruction in its proper performance. Rather than risk violation of the Shabbat, Raba cancelled the performance of the ceremonial mitzva (*Rosh Hashana* 29b).]

The mitzva of shofar is cathartic and redemptive. Yet because of a slight possibility of *hillul Shabbat* (desecration of the Shabbat), Rabah banned the blowing of the shofar. This means that according to all those authorities who maintain that in the Land of Israel Rosh Hashana is observed only one day, if it happened to coincide with Shabbat, according

to Rabah's decree there would be no shofar blown at all
that year. Similarly with the mitzva of lulav, Rabah banned
performance of the mitzva notwithstanding the fact that it is
a biblical commandment and that from the viewpoint of
ceremonial it is an exalted mitzva. In a clash of the ceremonial
with the discipline, the discipline wins out.

Adam and Eve

On Wednesday evening, December 22, 1971, Rabbi Soloveitchik addressed a joint audience of YC and Stern students at Stern College. The following is a synopsis of the Rav's remarks.

Tanakh is not only a book of history—it is also a book of the present and future. No matter who one is or where he is, the Bible speaks directly to him. It is regrettable that our approach to *Tanakh* is frequently limited to pulpit homiletics. Homiletics have their place, but frequently they result in the *Tanakh's* becoming a source of mere "vulgar common sense".

The Jewish weltanschauung is primarily concerned with man, his destiny, greatness, and smallness, as an individual and as a community. This paper will attempt to demonstrate that the anxieties and aspirations of modern man are described in the biblical accounts of creation. Every person must attempt to see himself in the biblical accounts.

Sefer B'reshit, as is well known, contains two accounts of the creation of man. The first is found at the very opening of the book and is placed with the account of the creation of the cosmos. Only at the end of the creation of the cosmos does the Torah tell us that God created man and blessed him. By contrast, the second account talks briefly of the creation of the cosmos and then passes on to a rather detailed discussion of man's creation and of his early experiences.

A closer examination of each account reveals basic differences. The first chapter's description of man's creation pictures man as almost an afterthought. His "birth" is mentioned in one breath with that of the animals. The second account is exclusively concerned with man. Similarly, the first chapter talks of man and woman (a biological

137

description), while the second talks of husband and wife (a social or ethical description).

The first chapter of Genesis is concerned with both the inorganic and organic cosmos. Man is described here because he too was created by God and constitutes part of the created universe. As he emerged, man was a child of nature---as was the brute of the field. It is not coincidental that on the same day that He created man, God created a very large part of the animal kingdom. In this context, man appears as a natural being. He shares a common biology with the animals.

"Naturalness" is a part of man, and for this reason Judaism has viewed man's biological existence not as a curse but as a challenge. Natural man has a potential for greatness which can only be actualized by man. Although he has both the talent and ability to develop himself, natural man frequently declines to accept the challenge. He prefers a nonreflective existence to a self-conscious one. Simplicity is to him preferable to complexity.

The second chapter of Genesis views man as a self-conscious being, about to give birth to himself. Man now reflects on his environment, something which man described in the first chapter can not do because he is part of the environment. As described in the second chapter, man struggles to free himself from the anonymity of merely being one member of a species. Man struggles to be unique—to be an individual.

Different names of God are used in describing the Creator in each chapter. The first account refers to *Elokim*, the second to *Ha-Shem Elokim*. Traditional sources explain this "change of name" as reflecting two different attributes of the Creator. *Elokim* conveys the idea of God as the engineer of the world and as its source of energy. Judaism has insisted on the centrality of revelation, and each attribute of the Creator must reveal itself to man. One can encounter

Elokim wherever one encounters beauty and life. In every
drop of water, in every seed and blossom—there one can
find *Elokim. Elokim* is to be found in nature, not in man.
The Psalmist describes this beautifully: "When I see the
heavens, the work of your fingers, the moon and the stars
which you prepared [I ask] What is man that you should
remember him." Man is insignificant when compared to the
cosmos—almost unworthy of mention.

In his *Kuzari*, Rabbi Yehuda Halevi points out that the
name *Ha-Shem* denotes an entirely different attribute—that
of a relationship between man and God. Not all men can
have this relationship with God; only those who challenge
the cosmos can bridge the otherwise infinite gap between
the human and the Divine. Man relates to God, not as a
part of the universe, but as a person. God, for his part,
befriends man as one befriends a stranger. God likes the
companionship of mortal, transient man. How does man
call to *Ha-Shem*? *Ha-Shem* is found in whatever is beautiful
and noble in man. In whatever is beautiful in man, *Ha-Shem*
is present. The *Hovot ha-L'vavot* says that in the selfless
love of a mother for an infant, one may find a reflection of
God's love for man.

Natural man lives as an instinctive biological being. His
existence is limited by natural laws with mathematical
boundaries. He can make no leaps and is pragmatic to the
extreme.

Only when man breaks with nature and rejects boundaries,
when he longs for boundlessness, when he dreams, can
man reach greatness. The man described in the second
chapter, who might be termed metaphysical man, reaches
for the infinite and yearns for happiness. While natural man
is complacent, metaphysical man is restless.

Judaism endorses the position of metaphysical man, albeit
with reservations. Verse eight reads, "And *Ha-Shem Elokim*

planted a Garden in the East, and he placed in it the man whom he had created" to watch the Garden and to work it.

Verse fifteen reads "And *Ha-Shem Elokim* took man, and He placed him [man] in the *Gan Eden*." At first glance, the second verse is redundant. Ibn Janach translates the first verse as stating the purpose of the Garden's creation. "God created the Garden in order to plant man there so that man might watch the Garden . . ." God has then tempted man to be stimulated and to challenge his environment.

Metaphysical man is pursued by two major fears—death and ignorance. Man wants to know all and he wants to live forever. The two trees which God planted were the antidotes for these two fears. Had man been patient, he would have been allowed to eat from these trees (why else were they created?), but man was impatient and forever lost his chance. Man had passed that boundary which must be placed on curiosity.

Fantasy, dreaming, knows no bounds. Left alone, man's curiosity would never have stopped after God's arousing it by placing man in the Garden with all of its temptations. Almost at the same time that man was placed in the Garden, God speaks to man, "And God spoke concerning man saying from all the trees of the Garden, you shall eat . . . But from the tree discerning good and evil . ." God here commanded man concerning man. Man's progress is called to a halt by a confrontation with the will of God. Man was told that he cannot exist without a moral imperative. Halakha, which represents God's will, has sounded a call for man to retreat. One who ignores the command, one who eats from all trees, is not metaphysical man but natural man simply living to gratify his every desire.

Natural man lives an outwardly directed existence. As long as the cosmos exists, he can never be lonely. The Bible does not describe natural man as being "*l'vado*" ("alone"). However, in the second chapter, man is described as being lonely. The Hebrew word for lonely, *l'vado*, has two meanings: (1) alone and (2) the subjective feeling of loneliness. One may be in Times Square, surrounded by people, and be lonely, although not alone. In fact, the presence of the crowd may intensify the loneliness.

Being lonely is a spiritual, human situation. Man is unique in feeling lonely—a feeling that he is not understood. No matter how much one loves another, they do not share a common destiny. Each man has a different view of God.

Natural man hates aloneness. People who know themselves, feel lonely. This feeling springs from depth of personality.

When God said of man, "It is not good that he is '*l'vado*,'" he did not refer to man's being alone. The first chapter amply deals with procreation and sexual desire. It is in that chapter that God blesses man with fruitfulness. God was concerned with man's need for a spiritual partner. Natural man did not need such a partner; metaphysical man did. Since it was the creation of the Garden which converted natural man into metaphysical man, the Torah tells us of the need for a partner only after it relates the creation of the Garden. But, instead of continuing with the actual creation of Eve, the Torah once again interrupts the natural flow of the narrative and tells us of the naming of the animals.

"And the man called the animals and the birds of the sky and the beasts of the field, but for the man He found no helpmate." Man here engaged in a scientific process of cognition and classification. In doing so, he introduced order into a seemingly orderless world. Nature is subject to such a classification process. It can be identified by function since it exhausts itself in its function, having no depth.

Man cannot be so classified. There is more to man than just a catalog of functions and actions. For man to be known, he must reveal himself (confess) to someone. God, too, cannot be fully described functionally; He must reveal Himself. But even the most honest person cannot fully reveal himself—since even he does not fully know himself.

When God says "I will make man an *ezer k'negdo*" *Ḥazal* interpreted "*k'negdo*" as an opponent. No matter how much a man and wife have in common, they remain two separate individuals. One may reveal himself to one's marriage partner, but at some point the "I" remains unrevealed. A tension exists between the two "I's." But in some mysterious way, the "I's" find solace in each other.

A marriage which reaches the depths of personality, in which each partner reveals his or her to the opposite partner, is an ontological community. Man has a need to communicate. Through communication man shares his joys, and confides his misery. It is only to the true friend that man can and will reveal himself. The marriage partner is such a friend. (Compare Rambam, commentary to *Avot* 1:6, "Obtain a friend.")

The continued existence of such a marriage partnership requires a commitment to a common goal—that goal, according to the Torah, must be the child.

"Therefore shall man leave his father and mother, and cleave to his wife, and they shall be one flesh." Rashi comments that "they shall be one flesh" refers to the child, which comes into existence only through husband and wife. The child converts the sexual act from a selfish exercise in self-gratification into a means of cementing the marital community. The partners become committed not merely to satisfying each other's physical needs, but in the development of the child as a member of the Jewish community.

On the Nature of Man

Before an overflow crowd gathered in the Nathan Lamport Auditorium of Yeshiva University, Rabbi Soloveitchik delivered his annual Yahrzeit lecture. The lecture was given on Sunday evening, March 7, 1971.

The story of creation of Adam is told twice in *parashat Bereshit* in order to reveal the dual aspects of man, which, because of his paradoxical nature, cannot be understood. In the first chapter man appears at the end of a long process of creation and his position is peripheral—signifying that man is only a creature in a cosmic world order. On the other hand, the story of creation related in the second chapter brings man from the circumference into the center; man becomes the culmination and objective of Creation and the Torah immediately engages in a narration of Adam's history—the opportunities offered him, his rebellion, punishment, and despair, the blessing bestowed upon him and the curses with which he was burdened. Man becomes a history-making being—*Va-y'hi l'nefesh ḥaya*—and the contradictions inherent in his manifest loyalty and faithfulness on one hand, and arrogant rebellion on the other, can only be fully understood on the basis of the second description of man's creation implied by the strange spelling of *va-yitzer.* *Ḥazal* took this to mean that man was created as a dual being and that he shares a double existential experience which is the source of an eternal identity crisis. In contradistinction to classical philosophy and Christian theology which speak of a division of man into body and soul, *Yahadut* is of the opinion that the significant division is within man's spiritual dimension itself; two souls reside within him. Furthermore, while classical philosophy and Christian theology consider the duality within man a result

143

of sin after Creation and that, therefore, the ideal state is one of existential monism, *Yahadut* sees the spiritual duality of man stamped in his nature of creation.

In order to further analyze the dichotomy of personality considered by *Yahadut*, it is necessary to introduce a passage from Rambam (*Hilkhot Yesodei ha-Torah* 2:1). "The Holy One, Blessed be He, knows His true being and knows it as it is . . . not with a knowledge extraneous to Himself as is our knowledge . . . for the Creator, knowledge and life are one from all aspects . . ." We can isolate the following motif from this passage: Any cognitive act presupposes a division into subject-knower and object known. When the subject and object are physically distinct this division is immediately realized. However, it is induced even by an act of self-cognition. Whenever something is predicated regarding some part or the whole of the subject, that part or even the whole of the subject-knower is objectified, and the cognitor is divided into subject and object. Thus, any knowledge of oneself is extraneous to the knower. However, this distinction between knower and known does not exist with respect to God, for any such distinction would imply a lack of Divine unity—*Hu ha-Yode'a v'Hu ha-Yadu'a*.

This estrangement of object and subject within man is, from the point of view of *Yahadut*, not only logical in nature but also experiential. Furthermore, this duality influences human behavior and emotions. Man belongs to a cosmic system and is united with his environment; he thus experiences existence as an object. As do all "objects," man exhibits the traits of (1) "openness due to vacuity" and (2) "responsiveness within a system." Man is open, because man-object has only a surface existence but no core and, therefore, no modesty, or *tz'niut*. Also, man-object exists only as an element of an all-inclusive order and cosmic drama, and to him reality is manifested by responsiveness to the system—and to exist means to work, produce, and interrelate with other elements of the system. Man-object does not exercise too much metaphysical, ethical freedom; his actions follow the collective pattern of his society, the system in which he lives. He is fair but not kind, honest but not compassionate, just but not loving. He is unemotional, precise, and ignorant of the world of individual conception.

On the other hand, man-subject is elusive and clandestine. He is not uniform because his depth allows him to hide—*va-yithabe ha-adam*. Unlike man-object, man-subject is not always fair because he displays extremism. His awareness is spiritual as opposed to sensual, and he is inexact and impatient with details, but he is sensitive to the grandeur of the whole. He is visionary and willful, and his "logic" is voluntaristic rather than rational.

Yahadut accepts both images of man and calls upon him to be aware of his antithetical character, to experience an ontological dialectic, and sometimes to act as subject, while at others, as object.

Man-object conceives of the system as served by man, and man-subject, convinced of his own worth, sees the system as serving man. *Yahadut* certainly recognizes the inner nobility, the *tzelem Elokim*, in man and the central position in the universe, and envisions the telos of man to be found within himself, rather than in the system in which he lives. Man was created as an individual and the covenant between God and *K'nesset Yisrael* is a private covenant with each and every Jew (compare Ramban, *Exodus, Aseret ha-Dibrot*). Jewish history is replete with examples of an intoxicated community berserk, abandoning all responsibility, moving inexorably toward a yawning abyss and being saved at "the twelfth hour" by a "crisis personality"—a lonely redeemer, man-subject (compare *Midrash Rabbah, Vayikra*, on *v'af gam zot*). However, *Yahadut* also recognizes the necessity of individual sacrifice for the community as a whole, and at times considers the *tzibbur* the raison d'etre of individual excellence. Esther was required to risk her life to save her coreligionists and *Ḥazal* attribute Moshe's greatness to the need of *K'nesset Yisrael* for a leader (compare *B'rakhot* 32a). Thus, although *Yahadut* appreciates the worth of the individual, still, often the teleology of man is to be found within the community. This dialectic is also seen in the total devotion to the rational logic of man-object with respect to the study of Torah (which allows no emotional consideration, prophetic intervention, or secret communications) while Jewish history, on the other hand, makes plain that the destiny of *k'lal Yisrael* has been decided, by a rational logic or an empirical set of rules, but rather by a postulated system of absolute norms indifferent to changing environment and modes of life. Basic historical decisions are not cleared with the practical intellect but are made by a mysterious will. This explains the great significance *Ḥazal* attached to *K'nesset Yisrael*'s pledge of "*Na'aseh v'nishmah*," of allegiance before deliberation. The dialectic of man is, then, transformed into the dialectic history of the Jewish people and is personified by Joseph, the great organizer and executive and yet still the great dreamer ("*ba'al ha-ḥalomot*"), even in maturity ("*va-yizkor Yosef et ha-ḥalomot*"). This dichotomy and iridescence of personality is symbolized by Joseph's multicolored suit.

Furthermore, the object-subject dialectic of insistence on both minute detail and emotional involvement is found throughout halakha. Although *Yahadut* embraced the philosophy of man-object and the fact that detailed physical performance is central in the attempt of halakha to elevate man by disciplined action, still, the Jew is enjoined to partake in the romance and adventure inherent in the quest for great spiritual heights. Experience, too, is of central importance in halakha as is exemplified by the mitzvot of *ahavat Ha-Shem*, *t'filla*, and *simha* on *Yom Tov*. The man subject has not been rejected, but, rather, the metaphysical dialectic has been translated into a halakhic dialectic of action and thought, deed and emotion, accomplishment and experience.

However, while man is intrinsically contradictory, opposite attributes of God, such as *hesed* and *g'vura*, are reconciled within Him—as *Hazal* interpreted *oseh shalom bim'romav*.

The duality of man and the unity of God heretofore examined is reflected in the *t'fillot* of Shabbat. At night the creation is described as in the first chapter of *B'reshit*, the creation of man-object subsumed under the general creation of the cosmos. In *Shaharit* the nobility and achievements of individual man-subject are stressed, as in *Yismah Moshe*. On the other hand, in *Minha* we note that God is one and in Him all contradictions are reconciled: *Ata ehad v'shimkha ehad*.

The Role of the Judge

What follows is a journalistic reconstruction of a lecture Rabbi Soloveitchik gave before the R.C.A. Annual Convention of June 1972.

The Torah writes in Exodus 18, "And it came to pass on the morrow, that Moses sat to judge the people; and the people stood about Moses from morning till evening." In his comment on this, Rashi, quoting the *Mekhilta*, says it was the day following *Yom ha-Kippurim*. Rashi also goes to great lengths to prove that the first time that Moses could have received Yitro was the day after Yom Kippur. Ramban and the *Mekhilta* just state it was that day. If so, the "morrow" is connected not to the coming of Yitro, as Ibn Ezra explains, but rather to Yom Kippur. What forced the commentaries to associate the judging of the people with the Day of Atonement?

First we must try to understand the meaning and implications of "on the morrow." Either we try to show the importance of this day by connecting it to the previous day, or the Torah could use "on the morrow" to contrast yesterday and today. According to the first view, today becomes an appendix of yesterday, and since yesterday had certain sanctity, so today. According to the second explanation, yesterday was a day of shame, while today is a day of honor and glory. For example, in Exodus 32 it says: "And it came to pass on the morrow and Moses said . . .You have sinned a great sin . . . And the people heard. . . and they mourned." Here the "on the morrow" contrasts the yesterday, a day of revelry, with the today, a day of regaining morality, reappraising what happened yesterday. It compares a day of repentance with a day of sin, of intoxication, of idol worship. Today is the rebirth; yesterday, the downfall. In a similar vein, we see that when the Torah describes the change the people

148

underwent following the incident of the spies, the *Ḥumash* states: "And they rose up early in the morning   we will go up to the place . . . for we have sinned." Again, the night before was one of black despair. All avenues of escape were cut off. In the morning, they lost their resignation, and a new spirit appeared. In the course of one night we find a change from tragedy to a rise in greatness. But as mentioned, the "morrow" has another connotation. The "yesterday" is singled out. No change is present, but rather a changeless identity, an experience not yet extinguished with the passage of time. The Jew refuses to let go of the sanctity he has attained. Today is nothing but a reflection of yesterday. "And you shall count unto you from the morrow after the Sabbath. . ." The day following Pesaḥ is no ordinary day, but rather a continuation of the beauty of the holiday. Many halakhot reflect this idea that awareness of sanctity does not wither with passage of time. For instance, the halakha of "adding to *kodesh* from *ḥol*" is a craving of a Jew for sanctity and a refusal to leave it.

We may now try to understand why *Ḥazal* always said it was the day after Yom Kippur. A Jew does not merely observe the Day of Atonement. He experiences it. The day lives on and accompanies man into the profane world. The philosophy of the day is not abandoned with *havdala*. Judgment and the human role in its application are not separable from Yom Kippur. Whenever Moses sat in judgment, it was the day after Yom Kippur for him. Why ? Most *dinei Torah* result not in strict halakhic decisions, but rather in *p'shara*, compromise. Compromise is the ideal legal solution, not strict adherence to legality. After the parties agree to compromise, the judge still exerts authority, as if it were a strict *p'sak*. The halakha requires a *kinyan* for compromise, which sets up the court as the authority. The judge is not an arbitrator. He is a *shofet*, judge. Compromise in this sense is not negotiation; it is a strict legal procedure, with the final outcome as close to the actual halakha as possible.

Compromise in Judaism is unique. In other legal systems, the judge may recommend compromise or arbitration. But by doing so, he relinquishes the right to settle the case. In Judaism compromise and strict legality are treated equally. The Talmud says it is a mitzva to compromise. All the halakhot applying to regular judgment apply to compromise as well; for instance, the prohibition against rendering judgment or hearing a case at night.

The philosophy of compromise is a twofold one. The Talmud in *Sanhedrin* quotes two verses as a source for compromise: "execute the judgment of truth and peace in your gates . . ." and "And David executed judgment and righteousness . . ." But why are two verses needed? Apparently two aspects exist. Normally, when peace exists, judgment does not, and vice versa. The Talmud thought peace and judgment and judgment and righteousness could be reconciled in compromise. Judaism knows of a charitable justice and of a justice combined with peace. A double goal is pursued which strict legality cannot accomplish. In secular courts, one of the parties involved must get hurt. Matters of litigation are resolved by victory for one and defeat for another. Victory and loss are total. Judaism does not acknowledge the principle of contradiction. Both parties may be right. "Two verses contradict each other till a third one comes and decides between them."[1] The third verse[2] does not say that one of the *p'sukim* is wrong. Both are accepted. Judaism may recognize both the thesis and the antithesis as true. A human being can never be completely right because he is finite. He is limited, and this spells imperfection, not only intellectually but morally as well. But if he can't be unreservedly right, he can also never be completely wrong. The two litigants appearing before the judge are both right and both wrong. Therefore Judaism tries to protect against total defeat. A controversy does not end in victory and humiliation; both participants give up something. This is judgment that is righteous.

Judgment and peace are the second goal. Common law is not concerned with resolving a feud. It resolves an issue. As a result of one victor and one loser, hatred deepens, animosity is intensified, the decision doesn't bring people together. Peace is left to the psychologist or social worker. Judaism brings peace by getting the litigants to retreat. The judge is changed from a magistrate to a teacher. The judge makes the litigants see that neither was totally right or wrong. This is not merely a judicial decision—it is enlightenment. Peace and friendship are restored. In the first chapter of *Pirkei Avot*, Judah ben Tabbai says, "Act not the part of the *orkhei ha-dayanim*, and when the parties to a cause stand before you let them be in your eyes as wicked, but when they have departed from your presence let them be regarded as innocent." Don't act like an omniscient, all-knowing, all-wise judge. Only God can have everything prepared before him in an orderly way, can see everything clearly. You don't know who is righteous and who is wicked. The *tanna* requires humility in justice. Before you render the decision both parties are guilty. Each must give something up by agreeing to compromise. After agreeing to compromise, both are right, and should be regarded as innocent.

This is the premise of Yom Kippur. Man can't always be right, he is a sinner. Yet he is not absolutely wrong, either. While practicing justice one must constantly be aware of the lesson and moral of Yom Kippur. Moses was taught this lesson by God. No one is right: *Mi yizke l'fanekha ba-din*—Who can stand before You in judgment? But on the other hand, he is not totally wicked: *Ata notein yad la-poshim*—You give help to the sinners. And it was only on the day following Yom Kippur, after he had learned this great lesson, that he felt capable of rendering justice.

In light of the analysis, a new conclusion, a redefinition of "judge" is necessary. The word judge denotes not only judicial or legal action, but points to the totality of human relationships.[1] The Greek and Latin translations of *Sefer Shoftim* refer to the book as the "Book of Judges." But this is incorrect. "And Deborah . . . judged Israel at that time . . . and the children of Israel came up to her for judgment." If she was only a judge, why did Deborah act like a queen? Nothing in the chapter mentions judging, rendering decisions, only acts of dedication to the nation. She chose the general to fight Sisera. Does a judge declare war? Apparently she was more than a judge. She determined the destiny of her people. She was a guide and a teacher of her people, not simply a judge. *Shoftim* is not the Book of Judges, but the Book of Leaders. We know that "Samuel judged . . ." He not only judged but he shaped the spiritual image of the people. Another proof is from our starting point. We know that Israel got *manna* and clothing. No commerce, industry or competition existed. If someone tried to take more manna than was allotted to him, it simply disappeared. If so, what did the people quarrel about? To what does "and Moses sat to judge the people" refer? But judge really denotes the total spectrum of human relationships beginning with leadership and leading to love. Civil justice wasn't needed. But an awesome need existed for leadership, teaching how to handle life, how to remove the problems of a slave mentality. So they clung to Moses. His mere presence was inspiring, That is why they stuck to him from morning till evening. They couldn't leave him.

Yitro misunderstood all this. He couldn't imagine a justice, friend, and teacher merged into one. He thought of Moses as a king, and that the people stood because protocol demanded it. It was distasteful to him that Moses was debasing the honor of the people by demanding that they stand before him. But Yitro was wrong. The standing was spontaneous. The Torah writes "va-ya'amod" when it mentions that the nation stood before Moses, but Yitro said "nitzav." What is the difference? "Omed" describes the physical posture of the people—standing—in contrast to Moses' physical posture—"he sat." "Nitzav" denotes standing with a sense of order. "Then Joseph could not restrain himself before all that stood by him." The Torah uses the word "nitzavim" here also because these subordinates were serving Joseph. Moses told his father-in-law that he was wrong. "I don't decide issues. I resolve conflicts between people," he told him.

The Torah writes, "And the people stood about Moses from morning till evening." Rashi quotes the *Mekhilta* as asking: "Is it possible to say this? But any judge that judges righteously for even one hour, the Torah considers it as if he learned Torah all day and as if he became a partner with the Almighty in creation, as it says, 'and there was evening and there was morning, one day.'" Rashi is telling us that to judge means to teach and that the impact of instruction by deeds is worth more than by mouth. One hour of productive deed is like a whole day of learning by mouth. But Rashi wasn't satisfied. What did the people learn by standing before Moses all day? They learned the idea of morning and evening. Ibn Ezra, Ramban, and Kimchi all explain that the word *erev* is derived from "to mix," as in *ta'arovet*. *Boker* is just the opposite. It is from the word *l'vaker*, to discriminate. At times nature is intelligible and cooperative, allowing us her resources. But at other times she is tough, destructive, stubborn, and unrecognizable. At times it is *erev*, mixing up, confusing, but it is also *boker*, with clarity and shape.

This dual reality is associated not only with science, but

with the human existence as well. Man has *erev* and *boker*, evening and morning, as well. We live, exist, enjoy, progress, learn, comprehend the meaning of life, and feel fulfillment. This is morning. We are cognizant of our continuous growth—whatever we didn't know yesterday we know today. However, man has the evening existence as well, a period of confusion, denial, and torture. This paradox is beautifully described by Rav Elazar Hakapar in the fourth chapter of *Pirkei Avot*: "and you live despite yourself, and despite yourself you will die . . ." You live by force, and you'll be liberated by death which is unwanted and compulsive. Judaism taught man both dimensions of life, to be grateful for the morning and faithful in the evening. "To proclaim your goodness in the morning, and your faithfulness at night." This is what Moses was teaching the people. If they understand the morning and evening they will be able to build the world. ". . . as if he were a partner with the Almighty in the creation, as it says and it was evening, and it was morning, one day."

Two *T'shuva* Lectures

The Rav delivers an annual *t'shuva* lecture before a large New York City Audience during the *Yamim Nora'im* period. What follows are two examples of these lectures. The first was given at the Hotel Americana on September 18, 1969. The second was presented at the 92nd Street Y on September 3, 1973.

In *Hilkhot T'shuva* 1:2, Rambam deals with the atonement achieved by the *sa'ir ha-mishtaleah*. He prefaces the discussion of the particular laws with a seemingly superfluous prologue: "The *sa'ir hamishtaleah*, since it is an atonement for all of Israel, the high priest recites *vidui* (confession) over it in the name of all of Israel." Since this law is an explicit verse in the Torah (Leviticus 16:21), the question arises: Why does Rambam quote this rather obvious law in this context? It would seem that in this law we can find the key to the efficacy of the *sa'ir* whose particulars are described in the remainder of the *halakha*.

To resolve these difficulties, the concept of *tzibbur*, of *k'lal Yisrael*, must first be analyzed. A *tzibbur* is more than a large conglomeration of individuals. It is a collective whole, a mysterious, invisible unit to which every Jew belongs. This is not only a kabbalistic and hasidic truism, but it has clear halakhic interpretations as well. Ramban says (in chapter 3 of *Hilkhot B'rakhot*) that even if all Jews get together and donate a sacrifice, it has the laws of a sacrifice of partners (for example, it requires *s'mikha*. See *M'nahot* 92a). Only if it comes from *t'rumat ha-lishka*, the collective fund belonging to the *tzibbur* as a whole, can a sacrifice be considered one of *k'lal Yisrael* as a unit rather than one of many individuals.

In light of this distinction, Rambam's introduction in *Hilkhot T'shuva* 1:2 becomes meaningful. Since the *sa'ir* is a *korban tzibbur*, the atonement which it attains is a collective one. Thus, an individual is not forgiven directly, but the atonement is granted to the *tzibbur* as a whole, and each individual partakes of this atonement as a member of the collective *k'lal*. The reason Rambam mentions this idea here is that in it lies the uniqueness of the *sa'ir*. All other means of atonement are directed to the individual and are thus totally ineffective without *t'shuva*. The *sa'ir*, however, atones for the *tzibbur* as a whole, and therefore is not dependent upon *t'shuva* of the individual.

This collective atonement, however, applies only to an individual who belongs to the *k'lal*. If one's connection to the *k'lal* is severed, then he cannot be granted the atonement which the *sa'ir* achieves for the *k'lal*. Therefore, if one is deserving of *karet* and is thereby excluded from the Jewish nation (*v'nikhrat mei'amo*), or if one is guilty of *mitat bet din*, which is a physical expulsion from the *k'lal*, he is denied the atonement of the *k'lal*. The apparent contradiction between *halakha* 2 and *halakha* 4 is now resolved. Immediate forgiveness based on *t'shuva* alone depends on the severity of the sin, and all violations of negative commandments are considered severe. The ineffectiveness of the *sa'ir*, however, does not depend on the severity of the sin per se, but on the destruction of the link between the sinner and *k'lal Yisrael*, and this only applies to *karet* and *mitat bet din*.

Having resolved the questions regarding the *sa'ir*, the problem of Yom Kippur may be analyzed. Is atonement on Yom Kippur granted to each Jew individually, or does God forgive the *k'lal* and each individual is forgiven as a member of the *k'lal*? The answer is found in the *b'rakha* recited on Yom Kippur: *melekh mohel sole'ah la-avonoteinu*, God Who forgives our sins—as individuals; *va-avonot amo bet Yisrael*, and the sins of the house of Israel—as a collective unit. The duality of the atonement of Yom Kippur is expressed by

Rambam as well (*Hilkhot T'shuva* 2:7): Yom Kippur is a time of *t'shuva* for the individual and the large group, and it is the culmination of forgiveness for Israel. Thus each Jew is granted direct atonement as an individual, and indirect atonement through the channel of the general *kappara* granted to the *k'lal*.

It has already been mentioned that Rambam considers *t'shuva* to be indispensable for the atonement of Yom Kippur. According to Rebbe (*Yoma* 85b) however, Yom Kippur itself atones without *t'shuva* as well. It seems inconceivable, though, that the institution of Yom Kippur can exist without *t'shuva*. A restatement of this problem is found in *Tosafot Yeshanim* (*Yoma* 85b): According to Rebbe, who holds that Yom Kippur atones without *t'shuva*, why was the temple destroyed? Weren't all our sins forgiven every year, notwithstanding the wickedness of the people? The answer given by *Tosafot* is that Yom Kippur without *t'shuva* provides only an incomplete atonement. The meaning of this answer can be defined along the lines mentioned earlier. Rebbe agrees that the individual *kappara* granted on Yom Kippur depends on *t'shuva*, like all other individual *kapparot*. Thus *t'shuva* is an essential element of Yom Kippur even according to Rebbe. But an incomplete *kappara* is attained without *t'shuva* because Yom Kippur also has a collective *kappara*, and in this regard, it resembles the *sa'ir* which does not require *t'shuva*. Rabbanan, whose opinion the Rambam accepts, hold that since Yom Kippur is primarily an individual *kappara*, one who spurns this *kappara* by not repenting is denied even the collective *kappara*, whereas the *sa'ir*, which is exclusively a collective *kappara*, does not depend upon *t'shuva* at all.

We have spoken of a *kapparat ha-k'lal*, in which case an individual achieves forgiveness merely by association with the *k'lal*. The only exceptions are those guilty of *karet* or *mitat bet din,* in the case of the *sa'ir,* and atheists, those who scoff at the Torah, and those who remain uncircumcised, in the case of Yom Kippur (according to Rebbe [*Yoma* 85b]). Yet though every Jew (except in the instances just mentioned) belongs to the *k'lal,* an individual should strengthen his link to the *k'lal,* and this can be accomplished in two ways.

The first is faith in the *k'lal.* We all have perfect faith in the coming of the Messiah. Yet Rambam (*Hilkhot T'shuva* 7:5) says that the redemption is contingent upon *t'shuva.* It logically follows, then, that one's faith in the Messiah can be no stronger than one's faith in the eventual *t'shuva* of *k'lal Yisrael,* so that the latter also becomes a cardinal principle of faith. Thus Rambam concludes that *halakha:* The Torah has promised that Yisrael will eventually do *t'shuva.* And one way of aligning oneself with the *k'lal* is by believing, despite the many physical and spiritual difficulties, in the future of the *k'lal.*

The second way takes into account the fact that *k'lal Yisrael* is not limited to those alive at given time, but includes all Jews from Avraham until the end of days. Thus on Yom Kippur we ask forgiveness through the medium of *Yizkor,* as well as by confessing our ancestor's sins (*anaḥnu va-avoteinu ḥatanu*). For even though a dead person cannot be granted individual *kappara,* the *kapparat ha-k'lal* includes all Jews in all generations. In view of this fact, one strengthens his link with the *k'lal* by joining the past and future of the Jews. And the best way of doing this is by observing and conveying the Jewish tradition particularly the very *Torah she-b'al Peh* which was given on Yom Kippur.

The T'shuva Process

How does the process of atonement (*kappara*) vis-à-vis repentance (*t'shuva*) differ today from the process of

atonement during the existence of the Holy Temple? For an
answer to this question, we must examine the text of *Hilkhot
T'shuva* 1:4. In *halakha* 1, Rambam describes the appropriate
sacrifices for particular sins and adds that those who are
required to offer their particular sacrifices cannot receive
atonement through their sacrifices until they repent. Similarly,
in the description of the atonement brought about through
the biblical scapegoat, Rambam stresses that the atonement
is only granted on condition that the sinner repent. It is
clear that repentance was necessary in the atonement process
during the time of the Holy Temple, but repentance was
not the agent that brought about atonement. Rather, the
appropriate sacrifices were the agents of atonement, while
repentance was only a condition necessary for atonement.

In *halakha* 3, Rambam explains the nature of repentance
today. "Today, since we don't have the Holy Temple or the
Altar of Atonement, there is [there remains] only repentance."
The explanation of this *halakha* and of what follows in the
rest of *halakhot* 2 and 4, is that repentance is no longer a
condition of atonement but rather the agent itself. Repentance
with the essence of Yom Kippur (*itzumo shel Yom Kippur*)
grant us our *kappara*.

In light of the above analysis, a puzzling statement of
Rabbi Akiva (*Yoma* 86b) can be understood. Rabbi Akiva
said, "Fortunate are you O Israel. Before whom do you
purify yourself? Before the one who purifies you, before
your Father in Heaven." What was Rabbi Akiva teaching us?
The answer lies in realizing that Rabbi Akiva was addressing
himself to the period after the destruction of the Temple.
The Jewish people, who had identified the atonement process
of Yom Kippur with the atonement process of its particular
sacrifices and the service of the High Priest, could not
understand how they would achieve purity and forgiveness
without the Temple.

Rabbi Akiva explained that atonement can be accomplished without the sacrifices and service of the High Priest. Indeed the Torah does mention and require all the sacrifices for atonement. However, this is a requirement only during the existence of the Temple. Today though, without the Temple, atonement is realized through repentance and the essence of Yom Kippur. We can further understand why Rabbi Akiva referred to God as "Your Father in Heaven." While the Temple was standing, a Jew could not approach God alone and achieve atonement. He needed to follow a strict set of operations, performed through an intermediary—a High Priest. God stood at a distance from man as a king who could not be reached by individuals. However, today, after the destruction of the Temple, man is able to approach God directly, and God without intermediates purifies and forgives man. Hence, God is referred to as "Your Father in Heaven!"

The process of redemption during the period between Rosh Hashana and Yom Kippur as explained in *Hilkhot T'shuva* 2:7,8 and 3:3,4) requires the repenter first (from Rosh Hashana) to increase in his performance of commandments and good deeds until Yom Kippur, and then to emerge in soul-searching repentance. Upon reflection, it would seem that the order should be reversed, first repentance and then good deeds. Why is it that we are told to start with the increase in performance of commandments and good deeds?

Actually, both of these approaches of repentance are correct, but are applicable to different types of people. The type of sinner whose sin stems from his arrogance and unwillingness to bend his will before the Almighty (referred to in the prayer book as *rishei aretz*) cannot start his return to God with good deeds. He must first reorient his thinking and humble himself before God. On the other hand, the type of sinner who sins because he is spineless and has no self-control (referred to in the prayer book as *b'nei basar*), who serves God—and not only God, but anyone or anything that leads him—may start his repentance with good deeds. He is aware of God's superiority but finds it difficult to follow God's ways. The good deeds purify him in readiness for his complete *t'shuva* on Yom Kippur.

In our repentance process God looks upon us all as "spineless sinners" rather than as "arrogant sinners" and requires us to start our repentance with good deeds and the performance of commandments.

Yom Kippur, then, expresses itself as a day of soul-searching repentance in contrast to Rosh Hashana which requires us to immerse ourselves in performing God's commandments and good deeds. Moreover, according to Rambam, it seems that Yom Kippur today is effective in granting us atonement only if we are entirely repentant, rather than repentant of particular sins. Rambam says (*Hilkhot T'shuva* 1:3) "The essence of the day [Yom Kippur] atones for all repenters." A person must be a repenter in total. This, too, does not distinguish Yom Kippur today from the Yom Kippur during the time of the Temple. In the time of the Temple, forgiveness could be granted for sins without necessitating forgiveness for others, since different sacrifices were offered for different sins.

To complete the concept of the repentance-atonement process we must investigate *Hilkhot T'shuva* 7:4,5,6. In *hilkhot* 4 and 6 Rambam describes the great purifying power of repentance. A person who, before repenting, was detestable in the eyes of God, is, after repenting, beloved and cherished by God. *Halakha* 5 seemingly interrupts the idea of *halakhot* 4 and 6 by expressing the link between repentance and redemption. The question arises of itself: Why did Rambam insert the *halakha* of repentance-redemption between the *halakhot* which describe the cathartic powers of repentance?

To find the link between these two ideas, we must understand the nature of redemption itself.

The redemption mentioned by Rambam is the redemption of the third and final Temple. How does this redemption distinguish itself from the redemption experienced as during the building of the second Temple? Rambam states (*Hilkhot M'lakhim* 11:1) that the future redemption will bring us back to the state of being that existed during the first Temple.

During the first Temple the consuming fire for the sacrifices was sent from heaven; the *Urim v'-Tumim* existed and the majesty of God was manifest. So will the situation be in the time of the third Temple. The second Temple, however, did not mark a complete reconstruction of the original Temple. The *Urim v'-Tumim* were gone. An imprint of exile remained.

The repentance process also has two types, one more complete than the other. In one type, the repenter still remains with an imprint of his sin. As a healthy man who has been made lame and has found his way back to health may still walk with a limp, so too does the repenter remain tarnished by his sin.

There exists, however, a second type of repentance that leads the repenter not to the level of the second Temple but to the level of the third. After the hard battle of returning to God, the repenter stands erect without the slightest trace of sin; he is closer to God than ever before.

Now the order of the *halakhot* in the *Mishneh Torah* becomes clear. Indeed, at the very point where Rambam describes the great cathartic powers of repentance, he includes the redemption-repentance link in order to indicate that the higher level of repentance is indeed accessible. This is the repentance that Yom Kippur affords and requires of us all—to repent completely and be restored close to God as in days of old.

The Seder Meal

This lecture, which deals with the significance of the Pesaḥ Seder, was delivered on March 30, 1969, to an audience of Yeshiva University students.

As a child, I [the Rav] vividly sensed the presence of God on two different occasions—on the night of Kol Nidrei (Yom Kippur) and at the Seder on the first two nights of Pesaḥ. The Seder is the prototype of the *se'uda* (meal), and the halakha has developed an ethic and an etiquette concerning the *se'uda*. Eating is a physiological function which is instinctive and mechanical—similar to the beast, insect, and plant. Thus, many philosophers stated that eating is a "disgraceful must," and many great men would not eat in public. Judaism, however, arrived at a different conclusion.

Although eating is a biological necessity, man and beast do not eat in a similar fashion. Judaism has redeemed eating from a coercive process into something meaningful and deliberate. There are two distinctions between the beastly eating process and the human one: (1) the beast eats alone, unaware of his neighbor, and (2) the beast cannot withdraw from its prey and retreat. In the approach of the Western World, man was not permitted to eat alone, since by nature man is a sociable being searching for companionship (the beast by contrast, needs no companion). The humanization of the eating process by modern man was realized by presenting the meal as a sociable process, thereby developing table mannerisms and various refinements. Elaborate and sumptuous dinners are commonplace. Eating is associated with aesthetics; whatever is beautiful is good, since beauty is a cathartic agent (according to Plato). This was the philosophy developed in the Orient and in the classical world.

However, Judaism maintains that the experience of beauty is not a redemptive process—it merely hypnotizes man, taking away his freedom. It robs man of the dignity that is expressed in freedom. Adam succumbed to the beauty of the tree, the falling angels succumbed to the beauty of man, and the *Dor ha-Midbar* (the Jews traveling through the desert with Moses) succumbed to the beauty of Moab. Since beauty does not humanize the eating process, there is a need for another redemptive course (Judaism has rejected the elaborate beautiful meal).

In Kabbalah, there are two movements: (1) *ḥesed* and (2) *g'vura*. The movement of *ḥesed* is a movement away from oneself, an advancement and a searching forward toward nonvisible vistas (*ḥesed* is identified with *hitpashtut*—a sense of revelation and openness). The movement of *g'vura* is an inward movement (*g'vura* is identified with *tzimtzum*—to recoil into oneself). whereas *ḥesed* implies a flight toward society, *g'vura* implies a human flight from society (it is the flight of the lonely one to the Lonely One). Man must learn to cope with both, depending upon the times.

The *ḥesed* community exemplifies the expression of kindness (a compulsive kindness), when one must give up things for others. The quantity of one's possessions is irrelevant to *ḥesed*. You must open up your existence and embrace the community on two different levels. On one level you share your material possessions (the binding force of the sharing community). On a second level, you must give up the "spiritual goods" that you have acquired through diligence and the study of Torah (the teaching community). Teaching is a gratuitous open existence wherein the spiritual millionaire gives up his "storage house."

Judaism believes that man must eat within a community of *ḥesed*-oriented people. It's not enough that the beastly function is raised to a human experience—it must be raised to a divine one. Only then do we have a redemptive process of this physiological act ("And you shall rejoice before the Eternal you God" [Deuteronomy 12:12])—a sense of *k'dusha* (holiness).

Zimun (invitation) prior to saying the grace after meals shows that one does not eat haphazardly with others as a conglomeration but as a cohesive unit. *Zimun* symbolizes the community of *hesed*.

On the first two nights of Pesah the Seder represents that type of *hesed* community. In the halakha we find that one should try to assure himself that two other people are with him at the Seder so that a community should participate in this event. When the Jews were freed from bondage, these two nights represent *hesed* in that *hesed* is a characteristic mark of the free man—the slave who is so concerned with himself cannot possibly join the *hesed* community. Only free people can think of others. God refers to the *hesed* community as "*am*" ("people" or "community," as in "bring forth my *am*" [Exodus 3:10]). The word "*am*" is derived from "*im*" (sharing). The concept of the *hesed* community is also symbolized by the Pascal Lamb—a community of concern and solidarity.

The *hesed* community is demonstrated at the beginning of the Seder with the recitation of *Ha Lahma Anya*, when we say the Jews in Egypt ate this matzah together and we therefore now invite all those in need to come and share our food with us. At the Seder, the blessing over the matzah, a broken matzah, is used to symbolize sharing.

The teaching community, also a *hesed* community, is an existential relationship between the master and his disciple. This too is seen in the Haggadah. Following Kiddush, the recitation of the Haggadah begins where we recite the history of the Jews in Egypt and their ultimate redemption. It begins with an inquiry (according to Aristotle, "the source of

knowledge is amazement"). The Haggadah isn't merely a
tale or a narrative of the events of the exodus. It is a
discourse and a study of the Jewish freedom from slavery.
We examine the highlights—it is a philosophy of the universal
and not of the particular. The Haggadah is really a study of
Torah (*talmud Torah*).

The Haggadah is directed toward the four sons, symbolizing
the idea that the teaching process must be geared to the
individual. Even the dull can and should be taught. Even
the very bright son can learn. Thus, the Torah community is
a didactic community within the realm of *ḥesed*.

On the nights of Pesaḥ, we must not only move forward
(the movement of *ḥesed*) but also recoil (the movement of
g'vura). We were commanded by God, "and none of you
shall go out from the entrance of his house until the morning"
(Exodus 12:22). We were commanded not to take revenge
upon our Egyptian taskmasters. When slaves rebel and
overturn their masters, in many cases the roles are merely
reversed and the slaves become the masters. God wanted
the Jews to present to the world a movement of *g'vura*—recoil,
which is the symbol of a truly great nation.

Insights into *M'gillat Esther*

Rabbi Soloveitchik delivered this annual Yahrzeit lecture to an unusually large crowd. The lecture, entitled "Insights into *M'gillat Esther*," was given in Lamport Auditorium on March 14, 1973.

The *M'gillah* and the story of Purim occurred at the sunset of the glorious day of prophecy. The nation as a whole was facing the sad reality of a nonprophetic future. During the Passover story (which happened during the prophetic era), Moses, the messenger of God, received clear, exact instructions how and what to do in fulfilling his mission. But Mordekhai and Esther, also messengers of God, living in a nonprophetic age, had no clear guidelines how to implement their goal. They had to use their own initiative, imagination, and ingenuity to carry out their divinely ordained "mission impossible": to save the nation from annihilation. This period of Esther is described as a period of *hester panim*, a time during which God seems to have hidden His Presence. All it really means is that He directs the action from the sidelines, from the shadows, without the glaring spotlights to pinpoint His involvement.

In every generation there are people whom God chooses to be His messengers, to become history makers. In the nonprophetic existence, they have to use much imagination and ingenuity to fulfill their mission. Whom does God choose? People who aren't simply individuals, but those in whom a multitude abides; individuals who contain within them a whole nation. Their role within Israel is that of the heart among the organs of the body. The heart is affected by anxiety, joy, fear, anger, and any other stresses to the body, yet it remains the hardiest and strongest of all the organs. The individuals whom God chooses are those who see themselves affected by whatever happens to the nation, who cry with the pain of Israel, and rejoice at its happy moments. (By extrapolation, this is also the role of Israel among the nations, according to the *Kuzari*.) Such individuals are more than single persons; they personify a whole nation within themselves. This is the concept of *shakul k'neged shishim ribo*, of one person being equal to the whole of Israel. Just as a nation doesn't die, so these unique individuals who represent the whole nation never really die. As long as *Am Yisrael ḥai*, then *David Melekh Yisrael ḥai v'kayam*. Haman realized that Mordekhai was such a person and that it would be futile to kill Mordekhai alone (3:6), for Mordekhai is the embodiment of the nation Israel and the nation is the extension of Mordekhai, so only total eradication of the whole nation could erase the power of Mordekhai. Such is the stuff from which Jewish leaders are made.

In the story of Purim, both Mordekhai and Esther were chosen by God to play crucial roles in saving the nation. From the time of Sara onward, women have been on equal, or even superior, footing with men in the history-making process. However, though both play equally important roles, they are different roles. A man cannot assume a woman's role and neither should a woman play a man's role. According to Judaism, men and women are spiritually and physically different, and though their complementary roles are of equal importance, they are fundamentally unique positions. Man initiates action while woman completes it. He is the theoretician while she put it in practice. He thinks in the abstract, she in pragmatic, realistic plans. Man is often a "schlemiel"; fortunately woman is crafty.

Mordekhai was to initiate the salvation of the Jewish nation. When the evil proclamations were posted, he didn't panic. Instead, he carefully analyzed the historical developments and came to the conclusion that Esther had been selected by God to save the nation. This "theory" made all the strange facts about Vashti, the feasts, and Esther's glorious rise to royalty fit into a coherent scheme. He knew that he was to initiate the rescue but that Esther was the one to fulfill it. He had two tasks ahead of him: (1) inform Esther of the events that had transpired (4:2–9) and (2) make Esther realize that she was charged by the Almighty for this task (4:13–14). His task as a teacher and educator was to inspire Esther to accept the responsibility. Up until this point, Mordekhai was the hero, the central figure, the leader who was giving orders and attempting to inspire Esther to follow his ideas. As soon as Esther agrees to take the challenge, we notice a sudden reversal of roles: Esther becomes the more prominent character and Mordekhai is assigned a less important role. She is now the master, giving instruction (4:16) which Mordekhai obeys submissively (4:17). After he fulfilled his task as initiator of the salvation, Esther, the woman, gains prominence as the one to actually implement the plan and use her own ingenuity to bring it to fruition. This is the cunning, the *bina y'teira* (*Nida* 45b) which was endowed to womankind.

In fact, Mordekhai had his own ideas about how to implement the rescue of the Jews. But it was the plan of the woman Esther that prevailed. Mordekhai wanted Esther to go immediately to the king and plead for the nation (4:8). Esther disagreed, feeling that slow, diplomatic channels were to be preferred. She made one wine party and then another, procrastinating for some seemingly unfathomable reason. However, if we delve into the personality of Aḥashverosh we will understand why Esther acted the way she did, and how the realities of the situation totally excluded the possibility of following Mordekhai's plan.

The king had a paranoid fear of an insurrection against the throne. The Talmud relates that he was not the legitimate heir to the kingdom, rather the son of the steward of the royal stables. His only connection with royalty was through his wife Vashti, daughter of Belshazzar. She obviously despised him as a social climber who lacked any royal grace and dignity. There was an underground movement to overthrow the government and restore the old order, as evidenced by the assassination attempt by Bigtan and Seresh. Aḥashverosh tried to "buy" the country's loyalty by making those lavish parties and inviting everyone to eat and drink and view his wealth and women. But this is all clearly the workings of a mind that feels very insecure and fears revolt. The absurd law (4:11) proclaiming death to anyone who entered the throne room without an appointment seems also to be an outgrowth of his paranoid fear of revolt or assassination. When Vashti publicly insults him, he was worried that if he should kill her this would inspire a revolution. M'mukhan (1:16–20) gave him the following brilliant analysis: "True, if you kill Vashti you may trigger a revolt, but if you allow her to survive after publicly insulting the king, then she will serve as a model for all the women of royal blood to insult their husbands." It was the custom in antiquity for the victor to marry the widow or daughter of the vanquished power. Thus, many of Aḥashverosh's officers had married women of the old order. "If they saw that the queen was not punished for her insolence, they too would start fighting their husbands and join the underground movement to restore the old order. The way to nip that in the bud is to execute Vashti." Thus M'mukhan, whom the Talmud tells us was Haman, gained the confidence of the paranoiac king, appearing as one who loyally defended the throne. Immediately following the assassination attempt by Bigtan and Seresh, we find that Haman was appointed prime minister. The king was really frightened, and in his paranoia he turned to the person who had proven his loyalty—M'mukhan (Haman)—and placed his faith in him.

Feeling slighted by Mordekhai, Haman decides to destroy the Jews. He plays on the king's paranoia by casting suspicion on the loyalty of the Jews. He tells the king (3:8) that the Jews are a unified nation, widely dispersed in the kingdom, with queer laws and customs. Being a strange nation, no one can guess whether they are planning a revolt. Should they decide to join the underground, their unity as well as their dispersion geographically could make the insurrection very successful. The king fell for this ploy and agreed to kill the Jews. When a paranoid lives in fear of an imaginary monster, all moral controls are abandoned. He has only one irresistible urge—to destroy. Esther understood all this very well and therefore could not agree to Mordekhai's plan of immediate action. Once Haman had succeeded in arousing in the king fear of Jewish revolt, no human power or pleading could dissuade him from destroying his imaginary enemies. In grappling with the realities of the situation it was a woman's mind, not a man's ideas, that was needed. Esther decided that the only way out would be to turn the tables on Haman and accuse him of plotting against the king. She procrastinated day after day, waiting to find a possible opening, a possible way to shatter the king's faith in his trusted prime minister. It seemed that only a miracle could weaken his trust and indeed a miracle happened: *Ba-laila ha-hu nad'da sh'nat ha-melekh* (6:1). This is the turning point in the whole story, the prime miracle. The most significant aspect of that night was not so much the king's new respect for Mordekhai, but his loss of confidence in Haman. You feel the king's malicious joy in taunting Haman while ordering him to honor "Mordekhai the Jew" (6:10). Whether it was Haman's mention of the royal crown (6:8) that made the king suspect his loyalty, or his failure to reward the king's benefactor Mordekhai, or the shifting perception of the universe in the mind of this paranoiac king, it was time for Esther to plant the seeds of distrust in his mind. This is the kind of subtle *hester panim* miracle, a change of mood in the mind of a deranged king, for which we give thanks to God on Purim. The next day, when Esther charges Haman with treason, the king willingly accepts the accusation. She explains to the king that had Haman really felt concern for the better interest of the king, he would have placed the Jews in forced labor camps, thereby keeping them under surveillance in a profitable setup. "But the villain is not concerned about the threat to the king" (7:4). By proposing to arm the countryside with weapons to kill the Jews, he was really making it much easier for the revolutionary elements of the population to organize their revolution. Esther made the king believe that Haman was plotting against the throne. The king's paranoia took over where Esther's words ceased. Upon returning from the garden to find Haman on the couch where Esther was lying he screams, "Do you even plan to seduce the queen while I am in the house?" (7:8). He was so convinced of Haman's treachery that everything he did was viewed through the lenses of his paranoia. He "saw" Haman not only planning the revolt but even trying to steal the queen! This was the ultimate sign of revolt. Haman's fate was sealed. The very strategy and the fate planned for the Jews now backfired on Haman and his associates.

This was exactly what Esther had planned. Notwithstanding the end of the Prophetic era, the young girl managed to fulfill the impossible mission given her by God. Mordekhai was the initiator, inspiring her to act, but she worked out the strategy herself and, with the help of God's miracle brought it to fruition. God's spirit descended upon her and subtly directed her actions (see Rashi's comment on 5:1). It was the Divine Spirit from its hiding place (*hester panim*) that really engineered the whole production—not by direct instructions, as in the prophetic era, but through the more delicate and subtle channels of the human mind.

Esther taught the Jewish people how to fast and how to pray (4:16). The inspired charismatic woman is superior to man in two ways: (1) applied practical action and (2) prayer. Hanah, the mother of Samuel, taught us all how to pray (*B'rakhot* 31). Though she herself can never be counted to a *minyan*, she is responsible for showing us how to confront God. While Hanah taught the individual person how to pray in a time of stress, Esther taught us how we should pray together as a nation at times of peril. It is strange that these two traits, pragmatic cunning and the ability to pray, are really opposite, and yet women excel in both. Cunning is to be found only in adults whose years of experience with life mature them to be able to correlate all the possible factors and devise a scheme of action. Immature people may be brilliant, but they cannot be policymakers. Prayer, on the other hand, is an art in which the child excels. An adult is too realistic, too cynical, too hardened by life. To truly pray you must believe the unbelievable and hope for the impossible. True prayer is also that which swells up from either total despair or complete ecstasy. The adult moderates his emotions and doesn't allow himself to "let loose" and go to the extremes of feeling. But a child gives free reign to the feelings of anger, happiness, disappointment, and joy. The child knows how to pray *mi-ma'amakim* ("out of the depths of despair"), and also how to sing a *shir hadash* ("a new song of rejoicing"). The Jew is asked to be an adult and a child at the same time. When called upon to act as a historymaker, as a messenger of God, one must act with maturity and cunning. But when one prays, he should shed his mature sophistication and let his overwhelming enthusiasm or unlimited grief pour out to God. One must hope for the impossible or know that nothing is impossible for God. These two opposing character traits find their most perfect reconciliation in womankind, symbolized to us by Queen Esther.

Purim Ideas

Speaking to an overflowing audience in the Nathan Lamport Auditorium of Yeshiva University, the Rav delivered this lecture on the dual character of Purim on March 4, 1974.

The Talmud (*M'gilla* 4a) establishes the requirement for the reading the *M'gilla* at night (Purim night) and its repetition during the day. Rabbi Yehoshua ben Levi quotes as a basis for this practice from the Twenty-second Psalm, which shows man in despair calling to God during the night and day. On the other, hand, Rabbi Ḥelbo in the name of Ulah quotes as a basis for this practice form the Thirtieth Psalm which expresses man's need to sing in glory to God.

Rabbi Yehoshua ben Levi identifies the reading of the *M'gilla* with petitioning of God from the depth of misery. Rabbi Ḥelbo identifies the *M'gilla* reading with a total thanksgiving to the Almighty. Its recitation is a jubilant expression of praise of God. In fact, both of these elements are found in the *M'gilla*. On the one hand the *M'gilla* represents the cries and supplications of distressed man before his creator. On the other hand, the *M'gilla* is also the expression of praise and song to God for redeeming His people .

Dialectical Character

The dialectical character of the *M'gilla* is also found within the Purim experience. It is well known that Purim is a day of gaiety and celebration. However, Purim also includes an element of prayer. It is a day of deep meditation. *Ḥazal*, aware of the difficulty of being involved in both elements of Purim simultaneously, instituted the Fast of Esther on the day preceding Purim. The Fast of Esther became the day of supplication and prayer, while Purim day became the day of celebration and thanksgiving. Yet, the Fast of Esther is an intrinsic part of the Purim experience and not an unrelated addendum.

In what metaphysical phenomenon is the dialectical aspect of Purim found? It is found in the human experience. Man is a frightened being, not in the psychological sense, but rather in the ontological and metaphysical sense. Man is a creature full of anxiety who, unlike the animal, lives not only in the perceptual reality—the present—but also experiences the realities of memory and anticipation.

Man's Fear

The reality of anticipation has man looking toward the future—his uncertainty breeding fright. The reality of anticipation leaves man in a constant state of need. Man cannot judge his state by his present circumstances alone, hence man always finds a constant need for and purpose in prayer. The uncertainty inherent in the human experience is reflected even in the prayer of thanksgiving—*Hallel*. *Hallel* is comprised of glorious praise for God, as reflected by Psalm 114 (*B'tzeit Yisrael*)—a psalm of praise to the Almighty for redeeming Israel from Egypt. Yet *Hallel* also includes fervent petitioning for Divine benevolence and protection as reflected in the cry *Ana Ha-Shem*! Please, God, save us!

Similarly Purim is also dual in character. The miracle of a doomed people being saved merited song and praise. However prayer and petitions were also in order since circumstances can change quickly. Aḥashverosh was liable to do away with Esther as he did with Vashti. The duality of Purim is based, then, on man's vulnerability.

Vulnerability of man is not simply a tragic truth but rather an ethical postulate. It gives rise to modesty and humility in man. How can a man rich in accomplishments, successful in all endeavors, be expected to be humble? How can he suppress his arrogance toward those who have failed in life?

The answer lies in man's vulnerability to change. Suddenly, without reason, a man can be cast down from the throne of success to the pit of despair. Man's vulnerability serves as a cathartic and ennobling factor. Humility then is the expression of man's awareness of his vulnerability.

Indeed the whole Purim miracle was possible because Mordekhai was aware of his nation's weakness. Had Mordekhai allowed arrogance to overcome him and tell everyone that he was the uncle of the queen, the miracle of Purim might not have taken place.

Reflected in Halakha

The concept of man's vulnerability is reflected in halakha as well. The numerous laws of safety in the Torah stem from the halakhic awareness that man cannot master his own fate. The concept of "making a fence around the Torah" through rabbinical ordinances, is also based on man's susceptibility to failure on the spiritual level. It is man's vulnerability which allows sinful man to stand before his creator in judgment. God, aware of all the forces to which man is exposed, approaches man with a spirit of forgiveness.

Man's exposure to fate, however, is not viewed as tragic or accidental in the eyes of the halakha. Unlike the Greeks, who felt that fate was the source of human tragedy, Judaism feels that fate has order and purpose.

The purpose of fate is usually above human comprehension. At times, however, man can see in retrospect the hand of God guiding fate. In analyzing an experience, man cannot ask why something occurred but he can ask what is to be derived from the experience.

Four Conclusions

What then is the message of the Purim experience? Purim leaves us with four conclusions. Firstly, man discovered that "all men are deceitful." Man, created in the image of God, can replace his divinity with total evil. Haman awakened the Jews to the fact that man can link up with Satan and become a total sinner, devoid of any divine spark. The concept of man-Satan is called by the Torah "Amalek". Amalek represents the incarnation of total evil in man. Amalek can be encountered in every generation. Hitler and Stalin represent in our generation the man-Satan. Amalek's destruction will only be realized in messianic time.

The second message of the Purim experience is that Amalek's hatred extends to everyone. His primary pre-occupation, however, is with the Jews. In causing suffering to the Jews he finds his greatest satisfaction. The origin of his hate is clouded under many names—social reform, economic reform, or religious necessity—however the hate is senseless and arbitrary. The Jews of Persia were awakened to the fact that someone hated them. The mere existence of the Jews disturbs the man-Satan.

The third conclusion of the Persian experience is that the hate of Amalek is all-embracing. All Jews, religious or assimilated, are hated by Amalek. At the time of the Purim drama many Jews were prominent citizens in Persia. Twelve thousand Jews were invited by Ahashverosh to his party. Haman hated all Jews and wanted all destroyed. The decentralized Jews were awakened to realize that they all share a common destiny. Though the Jews were divided by geographical boundaries, separated by language, and enjoying different lifestyles, they were all included within Haman's evil plans.

Inspiring Message

There is also an inspiring message arising out of the Purim story. Whenever Amalek rises against man, he is met in battle by a messenger of God. Just as Mordekhai and Esther rose up to defeat Haman, so too in all such moments of crisis man is used as an agent to implement God's scheme. In the Talmud (*Sanhedrin* 99a) Rabbi Hillel states "Israel has no Messiah, for they enjoyed him in the days of Hizkiah." Rabbi Yosef said "May God forgive him." This exchange may be understood in the following terms. Rabbi Hillel envisioned the redemption of Israel as possibly taking place without a human emissary of God.

Rabbi Yosef viewed such an outlook as bordering an heresy, and hence prayed that Rabbi Hillel might be forgiven. Intrinsic to the redemption process is the participation of a human redeemer. A titanic confrontation between the messenger of God and man-Satan must take place in order for redemption to occur.

Why though is this struggle a necessary element in the redemption process; as manifested clearly in our redemption from Egypt? The Jewish experience in Egypt underlies the morality of the Jew. The Jewish morality is a unique ethical code. It expresses itself in a warm and tender approach to man.

Tender Nature

This tender nature of the Jew is captured best in the word *rahmanut* which means love and sympathy. The word *rahmanut* is derived from the word *rahaman*, the possessor of love and compassion. The word *rahaman* carries with it a different meaning than the word *m'raheim* which means one who exercises love and sympathy. A *m'raheim* has the capacity to love or not to love to sympathize or not to sympathize.

A *rahaman* is compelled by his nature to be compassionate. He has no choice but to love. This quality of *rahmanut* describes the Jewish morality. The Jew has not only the capacity to love, but has the need to love.

How did the Jews acquire this trait of *rahmanut?* The Egypt experience internalized the trait of *rahmanut* within the Jewish people. Only an encounter with man-Satan can instill in man the capacity of *rahmanut.* The encounter of Egypt sufficed for the first commonwealth, but was revived once again through the Purim experience.

On the Love of Torah:
Impromptu Remarks at a Siyyum

On April 1, 1973, Rabbi Soloveitchik's *shiur* at Yeshiva University, completed learning the first chapter of *Hullin*. The Rav was asked at the time to say a few words in honor of the occasion. What follows is a reconstruction of his impromptu remarks explaining the custom of saying *hadran alakh*—we will return to study you again—which is recited upon the completion of learning a talmudic chapter or tractate.

The Jew unceasingly seeks, indeed craves, *k'dusha* (sanctity) and Torah. Ramban explains that the preface to the *shir shel yom* is always "Today is the first (second, third, and so forth) day in the Shabbat (cycle) because the Jew counts each day with longing, anxiously awaiting the arrival of Shabbat. In a similar vein, it is explained in *Sefer ha-Hinukh* that the counting of the *Omer* reflects the Jew's awareness that the goal of the Exodus from Egypt was the receiving of the Torah, and by counting the days the Jew demonstrates his impatient longing for Torah. Similarly, the mitzva of *tosefet Shabbat*, of ushering in the Sabbath some small time before its obligatory commencement at sunset, exemplifies the Jew's impatient yearning for *k'dusha*.

This search for *k'dusha* is really a search for The Holy One, *Ha-Kadosh Barukh Hu* Himself. Real *k'dusha* is found only when He "spreads the shelter of His peace (*sukkat shalom*)" over us.

The *Gemara* (*Yoma* 19b–20a) relates that once Yom Kippur was not properly observed in Nehardea and God explained that it was because of "*la-petah hatat roveitz*" (Genesis 4:7). In order to experience Yom Kippur properly adequate preparation is needed. We start preparing on Rosh Hodesh

181

Elul and gradually ready ourselves for Yom Kippur. During
Elul we must climb a very steep mountain. Yom Kippur is
the summit, the apex, the day of reconciliation between
God and man. One cannot cross immediately and directly
into *k'dusha*. At the entrance to *k'dusha* (*petah*), if there is
insufficient preparation, there is sin (*hatat*). In Nehardea
they were not prepared to experience the sanctity of the
day.

Muktze, which actually means something not prepared
from before Shabbat, may not be used on Shabbat, because
one must prepare for Shabbat. Preparation which is so
important for experiencing *k'dusha*, is also important for
talmud Torah.

In a certain sense what *k'dusha* is for the Jew, Torah is
for the *talmid hakham*. Torah should not just be an intellectual
pastime. True, one can enjoy the intellectual creativity involved
in *talmud Torah*, but *talmud Torah* should be an emotional
experience as well; one should feel a tremor when engaged
in it. The Torah should be seen not just as a book, but as a
living personality, a queen like the *Shabbat Malkita*, with
whom one can establish an I-thou relationship. In many
places the Torah is referred to as a personality, as for
example: "The Torah said before The Holy One Blessed Be
He." The study of Torah should be a dialogue, not a
monologue. If I look at the *Gemara* as simply paper and
print, as merely a text, I would never be creative; Torah is a
friend.

"Say to wisdom (Torah), thou art my sister" (Proverbs
7:4). If the *Gemara* is approached as a plain text you might
master it but you cannot be creative. To become a *lamdan*
you must look at the Torah as an individual—a living
personality. Then it becomes a part of you. I feel committed
to defend Rambam. Torah becomes a delight; it inspires
you. There is a feeling of joy at having something precious,

at having a treasure. But just as there is no Shabbat or Yom
Kippur without preparing and questing, so also is this true
concerning *talmud Torah.*

To be a *lamdan* requires *hatmada* and inquisitiveness
and curiosity. If I love someone I am inquisitive, I am
interested in him and in his plans.

If I were asked how an emotional experience can be had
through studying the laws of, for instance, monetary fines
and damages, I would say that it is true that the exterior of
Torah is formal and abstract, but behind the shell of conceptual
abstractions there is a great fire burning, giving warmth and
love, and one can love the Torah in turn with great passion.
When you apprehend the Torah as a personality, not just as
a book, it infiltrates your emotional as well as your intellectual
life. An *am ha'aretz* cannot have this experience, and one
cannot be a *lamdan* without it.

Blessed art Thou . . . Who has commanded us to be
involved (*la'asok*) in the words of the Torah." Torah is not
only to be studied but demands an all encompassing
involvement, *la'asok b'divrei Torah. Tosafot* (*B'rakhot* 11b,
s.v. *she-k'var*) asks why the blessing for Torah, recited once
in the morning, suffices for each time one learns during the
day no matter how many interruptions have taken place
(for example, one has gone to work), while the blessing for
residing in the Sukkah must be recited anew each time one
returns to the Sukkah after leaving it. They answer that
since the obligation of *talmud Torah* is continuous *v'hagita
bo yomam va-laila* (Joshua 1:8)—one is always conscious of
the mitzva. However, any discontinuity of awareness (*hesah
ha-da'at*) relating to the mitzva of sukkah effectively requires
that a new *b'rakha* be recited each time the observance of
the mitzva is terminated and then subsequently renewed.

Apparently there are two kinds of awareness according to
Tosafot. The first is an acute awareness; clearly this is lacking

when one thinks about other matters. The second is latent awareness and this awareness is still present even though one is engaged in other matters.

When a mother plays with her child there is an acute awareness of the child. But even when the mother works at a job or is distracted by some other activity, there is a natural, latent awareness of her child's existence. This latent awareness remains throughout her entire lifetime and can never be extinguished. It is expressed in commitment, devotion, and in a feeling of identification, a feeling that she and the baby are one. The infant is the center of gravity of the parent's lives. They feel they cannot live without their child.

The same is true with regard to Torah. There may not be an acute awareness of Torah for twenty-four hours each day. But the latent awareness never ceases. The injunction which forbids discontinuity of awareness from Torah is measured in terms of *pen yasuru mil'vav'khah* (lest Torah be forgotten from your heart [Deuteronomy 4:9]), not in terms of *pen yasuru milimod* (lest Torah not be studied). All the injunctions against *hesah ha-da'at* from Torah do not refer to a discontinuity of acute awareness. Rather they refer to a discontinuity of latent awareness, which, as already mentioned, is expressed in commitment, devotion, and self-identification with Torah. When even the latent awareness—the commitment to Torah—is forgotten and is dismissed from mind, then one is "worthy of death." This is the reason we say "*la'asok b'divrei Torah.*" "*La'asok*" implies that even when we are mentally involved with something else we are aware of Torah. This awareness of Torah should become part of one's "I-awareness." Just as I am always aware of my existence without having to walk around saying "I exist, I exist," so should I be aware of Torah.

If the blessing were "*lilmod Torah*" (to study Torah) and

related only to the cognitive act, then any discontinuity of the acute awareness of Torah would require that a blessing be recited every time Torah study commenced anew after a previous discontinuity just like the blessing for the Sukkah must be repeated with each new entry.

V'hagita (in the verse "*V'hagita bo yomam va-laila*"), refers not to the actual study of Torah, but to the mitzva of latent awareness of Torah. *Higayon* does not refer to thinking in the sense of pure intellectual detached thought Rather it refers to awareness of personal desires, wishes, and concerns; it refers to a deeply felt longing and questing, as in *v'hegyon libi* (Psalms 19:15), which refers to awareness of one's prayers and petitions. No matter how much involved one is in other matters, there should always be an awareness of the appreciation of Torah as the highest value.

For this reason when we make a *siyyum* we say *hadran alakh*—we still return to you. As far as acute awareness is concerned we are through, we are leaving this chapter. But the latent awareness remains and for that reason we still return again to learn *Hullin*. It is just like when a mother leaves her child and says "I'll be back." She does not say this merely to encourage the infant. She expresses a basic truth. A mother leaves only to return; otherwise she would never leave.

Da'atan alakh—in our latent awareness we are still committed to you.

V'da'atakh alan—we hope you won't forget us. We hope that you, the tractate, will also keep us in mind, and if we view the Torah as a friend, the Torah will indeed be able to watch over us.

Index

Bible

Commentators and Other Later works